IMAGES · OF · PREHISTORY

IMAGES · OF · PREHISTORY

Text by Peter Fowler · Photographs by Mick Sharp

CAMBRIDGE UNIVERSITY PRESS

CAMBRIDGE · NEW YORK · PORT CHESTER · MELBOURNE · SYDNEY

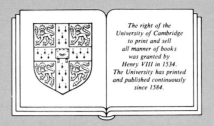

from MS
for Dorothy and Walter
who must have wondered what on earth I was playing at,
and for Jean,
who knew only too well

from PJF
for Rachel, Ruth and Brigid
who have variously, and often voluntarily,
visited and viewed the monuments of my images

Published by the Press Syndicate of the University of Cambridge

The Pitt Building, Trumpington Street, Cambridge CB2 1RP

40 West 20th Street, New York, NY 10011, USA

10 Stamford Road, Oakleigh, Melbourne 3166, Australia

© Cambridge University Press 1990

© Photographs Mick Sharp 1990

First published 1990

Printed in Great Britain by BAS Printers Limited, Over Wallop, Hants

Designed by Paul Oldman

British Library cataloguing in publication data

Images of prehistory: views of early Britain.

1. Great Britain. Prehistoric antiquities

I. Title   II. Fowler, Peter *1936*   III. Sharp, Mick *1952*

936.101

Library of Congress cataloging in publication data

Fowler, P.J.

Images of prehistory: views of early Britain/Peter Fowler:

photographs by Mick Sharp

        p.   cm.

Includes index.

ISBN 0521 35646 6

1. Man, Prehistoric – Great Britain – Pictorial works.

2. Great Britain – Antiquities – Pictorial works.

I. Sharp, Mick.   II. Title

GN805.F69 1990

936.1'0022'2 – dc20   90–1976   CIP

ISBN 0 521 35646 6 hardback   VN

Contents

Foreword

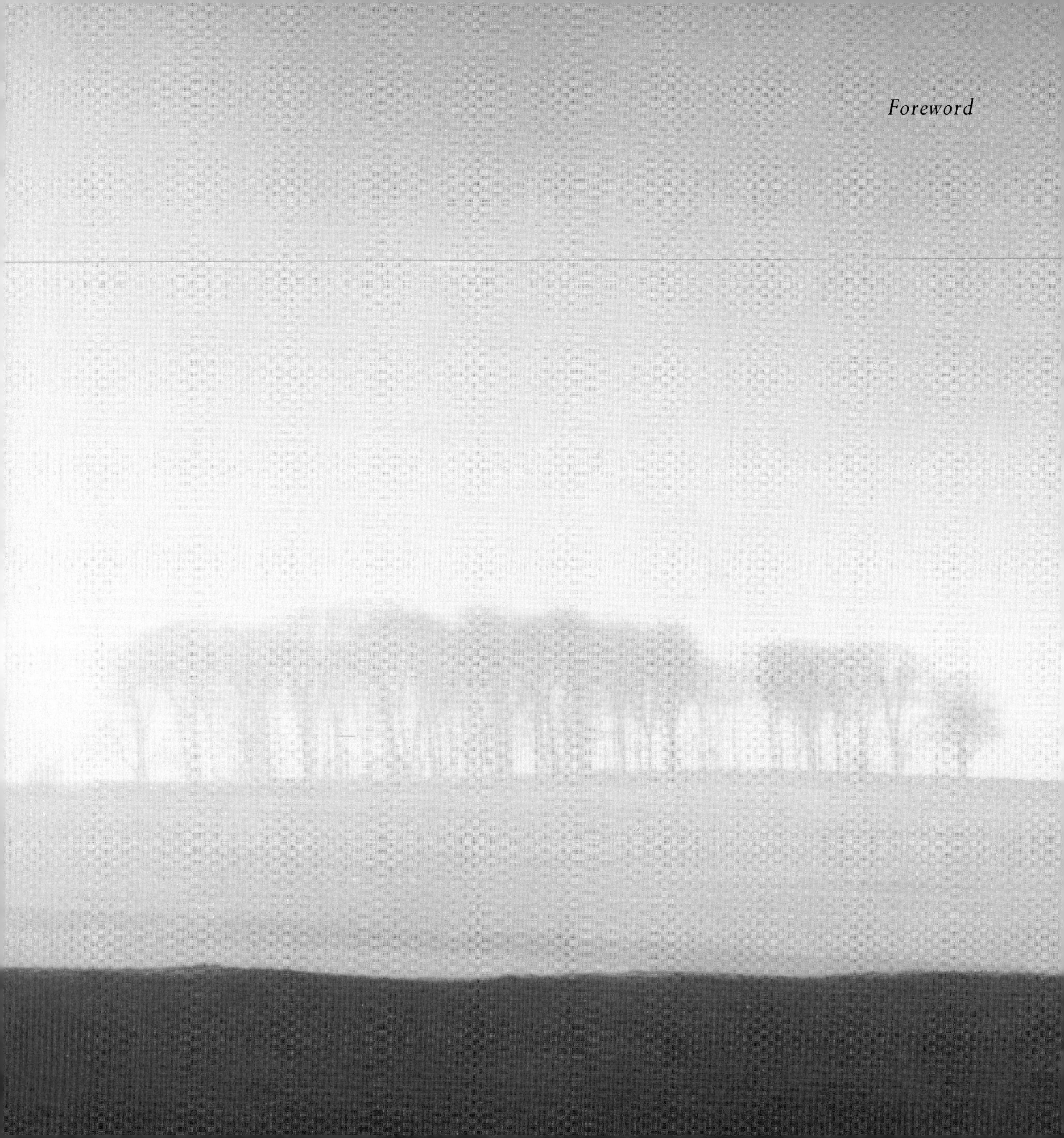

The inspiration for *Images of Prehistory* lies in the doggedly pursued and vivid photography undertaken over many years by my collaborator Mick Sharp. Alone, during the 1970s, he built up an impressive collection, often following in the footsteps of earlier antiquaries to both well-known and remote megalithic sites: the standing stones and circles, the burial places, sometimes the ruinous living places of our ancestors. Progressively he extended the number of sites he visited and then, one day, a clutch of his prints came into my hands. A collaboration developed, first over the idea of this book which began to influence the direction of Sharp's photography and then, through 1987–8, in the field as we ranged widely over Britain. During this last phase we deliberately attempted to expand the scope of his portfolio in areas and with types of sites on which he had not previously concentrated.

The result here, the fruits of painful selection from a thousand and more prints, is unavoidably, and unapologetically, personal. Any selection would be incomplete in one way or another and by definition we could only photograph what is there to be photographed – and beyond that only what we were physically able to reach. It is the material itself which took us mainly west and north for, by and large, that is where so much was originally built in stone. There too, on the hills and moors, the windswept headlands and lonely islands, our ancestors' use of the land over the last two thousand years has tended to be less intensive, so structures with a built-in bias to survival anyway because of their material have been relatively kindly treated; sheep do not eat megaliths.

To east and south, inevitably under-represented here, prehistoric people were just as numerous; more so in the last thousand years BC. There they tended to build of wood and earth, however, and continual cultivation of the land since then has erased the remains of such less solid structures. Not always: many a southern hilltop swells with now-grassy banks remnant from defences long defunct by the time of Christ. But in an area where the natural building materials were clay and gravel, chalk, wood and straw, structures contained a potential for collapse and decay. They were erected too along river valleys and on the shallow light soils of the downs where arable farming has tended to persist and prosper, not least in the last thirty years. In this lowland zone, then, most of the equivalents to what we portray here from the stony west and north have been flattened so that there is now often very little to see at ground level.

The images presented here cannot reflect the whole picture. We have not set out to present a prehistory of Britain nor do we claim a balanced portrayal of the country's prehistoric monuments. Yet, precisely because our portrayal is skewed, it contains an inner truth; it is, in the late twentieth century, a reasonably accurate reflection of that which has survived for at least two millennia. By definition, what we portray is visible and, in most cases, visitable. We would emphasise, however, that our sample is a very small one in relation to the extent and quantity of sites that still survive in upland Britain. This is the rationale for taking four areas where we have been able to illustrate in a little more detail the range and density of prehistoric survivals still existing in the present landscape. Even there, however, we have had to be selective. What we show is but a fraction of what is known; that amount in turn is but a fraction of what is still to be discovered, let alone understood.

These are aspects of the past today – its relativity and its dynamism – that an interested but innocent visitor to a preserved site can find difficult to grasp. It is a dimension conveniently ignored by those, for example, who would persuade us of the significance of imaginary straight lines across our maps supposedly revealing Great, but sadly spurious, Truths. To discover how people behaved in prehistory is a legitimate, intellectually demanding and intriguing quest to be conducted by rational inference from the surviving monuments and what remains of their context; but that funds of lost knowledge are somehow lurking in these monuments for our benefit if we can but unlock a key to the past seems unlikely. Prehistoric people undoubtedly operated within different parameters from the British today but we very much doubt whether they had access to any sort of higher truth now denied us.

To say as much may disappoint some but it should not be taken as denying the value of studying prehistory. Our lives can only be made richer by a well-founded knowledge of where we have come from. Furthermore, deeper understanding of the contemporary countryside can come from a knowledge of and sympathy with the achievements of prehistoric peoples. Such understanding, sadly lacking at present, is of considerable relevance to issues of land management, tourism and leisure, and education. In the last, the increasing exclusion of prehistory from school and college syllabuses appears to stem from either ignorance or deliberate conspiracy. This downgrading is remarkable at a time when adult interest as reflected, for example, in television viewing figures, the numbers of visitors to museums and historic sites, and book club membership, continues at a high level. Perhaps prehistory is not exciting enough for the classroom, perhaps it does not contain enough facts and dates about Great British Events for the '1066 and All That' school of history. Its demanding detective work, however, its use of inter-disciplinary evidence, and its work-places in the laboratory and in the field seem ideally suited to develop a whole range of skills and interests. But perhaps it is not perceived as 'useful'; perhaps, and maybe this amounts to the same thing, the study of prehistory is not producing the 'right' sort of answers for the sort of society it is deemed we ought to be in the late twentieth century.

We portray no great truths here, nor do we perceive phantoms or inner meanings in our subjects. We visited the monuments, recorded, and wondered. Personally, my reaction is an increased respect, not just for the monuments themselves, visually, structurally and as storehouses of information for questions not yet conceived, but more particularly for the people, my ancestors in an ancient land, whose struggles and aspirations these structures embody. We would not, however, urge any particular view of the past on those who pause at these pictures or tour the sites and landscapes we depict. Experience unconsciously colours my interpretative views, expressed in words but inevitably transient reflections; Mick Sharp's black and white views, like the anonymous monuments, should last a little longer.

Peter Fowler

LINEAMENTS OF PREHISTORIC BRITAIN

The images in this book are based on works made and used by people during the last four thousand years before the birth of Christ. That may seem a remote period but it ends only two thousand years ago, about thirty-five generations back from our own time. Though the core of the volume covers a period twice as long up to the arrival of the Romans in Britain as we are now distant from them, those four millennia fall in fact at the end of nearly half a million years during which *Homo sapiens* had been living in these islands. In the perspective of human affairs, they constitute a relatively short period. One can accordingly argue that the 'later prehistory' with which we are primarily concerned was neither remote nor very long and, further, that what happened then is directly relevant to all of us today.

By any standard, the last four millennia BC in Britain were a remarkable time. It was not a great chasm of years in which nothing happened; nor was it a time which we can now learn little about or from. Compared to the hundreds of thousands of years in which humans had been living here previously, this period was marked by the invention, introduction and application, quite suddenly, of a whole range of technologies in a great spurt of innovation and activity; and compared to what followed in the Roman period and afterwards, the later prehistoric millennia laid the foundations for a great deal. Up until the seventeenth and eighteenth centuries AD, in technological terms the Roman and medieval worlds were different essentially in the scale of their application of what was already being practised by prehistoric man. It was only with another technological spurt in post-medieval times in western Europe, leading to the machine-based world of today, that the order of change altered significantly from what it had been for some seventeen centuries since the arrival of the Roman army of conquest in 43 AD.

Of course, as the events of that year and the following decades showed, the prehistoric Britons had not developed either their technology of war or their social fabric sufficiently to enable them to confront the invaders on equal terms in the military arena. Further, as the material culture of the Romanised world developed in parts of Britain during the next three and a half centuries, many things were, and were seen to be, different. New types of building and new building materials were used; the arch, unknown here previously, was introduced and so too was central heating. Water power was harnessed in a way not previously known; the Britons did not have water-mills and, basically

Robin Hood's Cave is the largest of twenty caves along a narrow limestone gorge immediately east of Creswell, just on the Derbyshire side of the county boundary with Nottinghamshire. The name reflects the local admiration for a national hero, rather as King Arthur's also occurs widely. It has nothing to do with the long sequence of prehistoric human and animal activity archaeologically attested along Creswell Crags over some 40,000 years up to the Neolithic period (c 4000–2000 BC) with which our photographic images begin in earnest. This is one of five entrances.

through lack of the cog-wheel, machinery was unknown in prehistoric Britain. Under the Romans a national road network was planned and built, so permanently that parts of it are still in use. Above all, the Romans planted towns which we would recognise as such, truly urban settlements different in nature from the conglomerations of British populations which had previously existed.

So there were and are differences between prehistory and later, not least a string of technological advances from the Roman period onwards; but the latter list is short. Look at the achievement of those last four prehistoric millennia, comparing it in particular with what went before. Very briefly, Man learnt to farm, probably the single most significant development in human history; he learnt to build, went some way towards solving the problem of roofing built space and began to develop the concept of architecture; he learnt to exploit the mineral resources of his environment enabling him to become stone-mason, sculptor, and metal-worker in copper, bronze, iron, gold, silver and lead; he invented the wheel, pottery, carpentry, all the basic tools needed for an agrarian way of life, as well as techniques of land manage-

'Enclosures and hut circles': thus the Ordnance Survey's Tourist Map of Dartmoor describes this area about a kilometre south-east of Rippon Tor. On the ground the visitor can see, at best, only banks and stones in no apparent order. From the air, however, the camera both records more and conveys an image of pattern, here of a rectilinear field system interlaced with lanes and at least one settlement (right centre). This organised landscape of the 2nd millenium BC is now dead in the sense that it no longer supports farmers and their families; but as scientific evidence, preserved accidentally by non-intensive land use over the last three thousand years, it is priceless.

Much of the landscape evidence for prehistoric Britain is not in fact visible most of the time; it has been razed and buried, now appearing seasonally and differentially, only to be appreciated from above and through patient photographic recording of the fleeting evidence year by year. This area of intensive agriculture between Northmoor and Standlake 10 km west-south-west of Oxford is a total blank on the Ordnance Survey map, yet it has been intensively settled and farmed in the past as the evidence of crop-marks shows. Best seen from the air, crop-marks are a reflection of differential crop-growth occasioned by disturbances to the subsoil, here gravel dug into by pits and ditches mainly in late prehistoric and Roman times. The picture, typical of river gravels throughout Britain, is both incomplete and complex; clearly many phases are witnessed, both overall and in individual groupings of features. Excavation would show the story to be even more complicated.

(Opposite) Many well-educated people would probably claim to know well one of the most famous fields in England, The Parks, Oxford—yet it is much more than an idyllic piece of scenery. In the expanse of tree-studded grass is the University cricket ground, demarcated (lower centre) as a sub-circular area around the square (the dark rectangle) with the pavilion to the left. Underlying the whole field are flattened archaeological features, typical of a Thames valley gravel terrace, photographed here in the 1976 drought when they were showing dark as richer herbage among parched grass (as is the cricket square which has been watered). Second millennium BC ditched burial mounds align west of the pavilion, late prehistoric/Romano-British settlements cluster around it and just beyond the central tree-clump, while the rash of spots from behind the pavilion towards the western Park entrance probably consists of late prehistoric storage pits, perhaps later graves and possibly even some Anglo-Saxon house-sites.

ment such as land-allotment, forestry and manuring; he also invented astronomy, geometry, civil engineering, organised religion, and some form of local government to cope with the tens if not hundreds of thousands of people in any one settlement area. He also developed the practice of riverine and coastal boating and the cross-Channel shipping needed for trade. From Gaul, he imported the idea of coinage, mints and cash. He became an artist, producing in particular some of the most wonderful decorated metalwork ever made in Britain.

The list could continue but it should have made the point. With a few significant exceptions, by 1 BC prehistoric people had invented or at least initiated many of the technological developments which were still underpinning the European way of life in 1600 AD. The one really significant absentee from the list identifies one of the great cultural differences between the pre-Roman period and the first Elizabethan era. As far as we know, prehistoric people in Britain could not write.

This means that we have no direct documentary evidence from a prehistoric person's own hand; not a single prehistoric voice, not a word, is available for us to study. For us today, heirs to the literate tradition of the Classical world and Christianity, and with a post-Renaissance scholarship couched almost entirely in the written word, the absence of documentary evidence places a huge barrier between prehistoric times and our understanding of it. Even today, some historians find the barrier impenetrable and methods of tackling it academically unacceptable. Despite the admitted difficulties of trying to learn about the undocumented past, such a viewpoint is fundamentally negative; for the approaches of archaeology, anthropology, geography and sociology can tell us much and a whole range of applied techniques from the sciences can tell us more. What is extremely difficult to produce is conventional narrative history: prehistory has no chronicles, diaries, or sequential records from institutions such as government. Nor does it produce individuals, so our perception of it is doubly handicapped in that it is highlighted neither by stories nor heroes. This point is emphasised by the last century or so of 'prehistory' before the Claudian invasion when, from coins and Classical sources, for the first time we are given names and events and, in conventional terms, history becomes more soundly based and 'more interesting'.

Such illiteracy was both benison and constraint. Prehistoric peoples surely developed and maintained an aspect of cultural behaviour which

Chillingham Park, Northumberland, is a medieval emparkment, its stone wall surrounding some 148 hectares of rough grazing and woodland. The herd of wild cattle trapped within it has survived through inbreeding alone. Here, one of the cows stands in typical bracken-infested surroundings, showing the characteristic white coat, black eyes, blue-spotted neck and dark brown muzzle of the breed, and the incurving horn-tips of her sex. In April 1947, only 13 animals (8 cows, 5 bulls) had survived the severe winter; by April 1990, the herd contained 17 bulls and 29 cows, with 9 calves having been born over the previous year.

we have lost: that strong oral tradition of practical wisdom and narrative expression reflected in some Early English writings and heard fragmentarily even into this century among survivors of pre-First World War East Anglian communities recorded by George Ewart Evans.

For the years before the addition of written sources to the range of our evidence, however, we have to learn to read the monuments and the landscape. We have to learn to devise, write and appreciate a different sort of history. We have to observe, record in detail, and infer. Such an approach is not so different from that of conventional history; the distinction is that we deal not with the written word but with artefacts as our primary evidence, these artefacts ranging from the landscape to microscopic specks of charcoal. The limitations thereafter involve in particular the thought of prehistoric people, which can but be largely guesswork on our part and, consequently, such elements of their life as belief and motivation; and more generally such matters as social organisation where the absence of records can never allow us to know, for example, about land tenure, legal constraints, or kinship relations

This book of photographs illustrates part of the primary evidence from later prehistory. It is not the evidence itself – that consists in the

These are not ancient tools but surrogates for part of the tool kit available to prehistoric man before he developed metal equipment. They were made and used in 1960 to build part of the experimental earthwork on Overton Down, Wiltshire. To try to establish some basic figures for possible prehistoric work-rates using this equipment, part of the experiment, obviously with severe limitations, was to use it in timed spells to dig out a ditch from solid chalk bedrock and pile up the spoil into a bank. The antler pick was effective at breaking up the chalk but the ox shoulder-blade, supposedly a shovel, proved more useful for scraping the chalk together and then into a basket. The items shown are now themselves in a museum.

West from Glastonbury Tor, the Somerset Levels are framed to the south by the Polden Hills and to the north by Mendip. Brent Knoll rises (right centre) on the horizon near the eastern shore of the Bristol Channel where dunes and mudbanks impede the sluggish freshwater drainage from the basin of the Levels. Minor islands such as Westhay rise a few metres above the surrounding soggy, floristically rich pastures, now succumbing to peat-extraction and arable. There may seem little of prehistoric interest in such a landscape but in fact the natural circumstances, exploited over millennia by people living off the diverse flora and fauna have preserved waterlogged in peat organic evidence ranging from pollen grains to large timbers. Numerous wooden trackways crossed the area from the 4th millennium BC onwards as water levels rose and fell; and settlements of the last centuries BC survived at Meare and near Glastonbury itself to be rediscovered from the 1880s.

The prevalence of wood in prehistoric life is exemplified in this detail of Butser Ancient Farm, Hampshire. High woven fencing separates a paddock from a log building as part of a reconstruction of a working farm of c 300 BC. The management of woodland to produce material for such structures is attested three thousand years earlier in the Somerset Levels and continued into this century. The four-year-old mouflon ram, one of the Butser flock of rare breeds, descends from the sheep domesticated early in the transformation to farming in the Near East; wild contemporaries survive in Corsica and Sardinia.

monuments and their landscapes in the field – nor is it, in any scientific sense, a record of that evidence. Our collection is subjective: in what has survived, and been deliberately preserved, to be available for photography; in what we have chosen to photograph from what is available; in the particular views and angles that we have used; and, finally, in this particular selection for publication of what we have photographed. Photographs and text describe this evidence, together combining, not least by using inference, to create an image, our image, of what we see and perceive.

This perception embraces an awareness of what we cannot present here. That notably includes the dynamics of landscape change as vividly captured in air photographs of the flattened and normally invisible sites and landscapes of later prehistory over lowland Britain. It is a perception, however, which does embrace, eclectically perhaps rather than consistently, many factors other than the strictly archaeological. Such elements drawn from geology, climatology, botany, folklore, local history and not least, recent treatment and current use of monuments and the landscape, variously help with perception, understanding and enjoyment.

At one level, for instance, we see a not unappealing photograph of an obvious 'cow' and, at second glance, infer from the bulky and horned appearance of the image that it looks like a bull. The angle and quality of the photograph may suggest to the biblically-minded overtones of a bull in a thicket while the white sheen on its coat may possibly suggest to the literary-minded shades of Henry Tegner's *White Cattle of Chillingham*. The beast is in fact a lone cow of the Chillingham herd, enclosed in Northumbrian parkland since the fourteenth century and now a re-markable historical survival from the pre-Improvement era in the eighteenth century and later.

Beyond this, we see four other layers of significance embedded in this one beast. It represents, indeed partly contains, a gene bank of great scientific interest. It symbolises, in its rarity and in being wild, Man's achievement in domesticating selected parts of the animal kingdom and, in particular, the bovines; physically, it is similar to the cattle prehis-toric man had to contend with, for it is close to the ubiquitous *Bos longi-frons*, familiar in thousands of bones from late prehistoric sites. It in-habits a medieval parkland which, as well as its later imported exotic trees, contains pre-medieval plant communities affording us a glimpse of the natural environment of prehistoric people. And finally, at a very different level, it is part of the herd of Chillingham cattle, now a high quality and increasingly popular tourist attraction, the management of which raises interesting questions about access to 'our heritage' – in this case not just live but wild too.

Though a straightforward image in one respect, the Chillingham beast therefore raises many points of perception and presentation. Such underlie not only the following pages but prehistory itself. The monu-ments, the landscapes, they are all 'real' in that they exist and are photo-graphable; but their significance is largely a matter of individual percep-tion and, in the case of prehistory, this involves the creation in our own minds of an entirely intellectual construct. Without that framework, these man-made creations are but things, inert and devoid of meaning or, at best, inexplicable except as the works of the Devil, Woden, giants, or little green men from outer space. That we have over the last two hundred years created the lineaments of prehistory from a rational exercise of three of humanity's strong points – curiosity, observation and deduction – is the best possible compliment we could pay to our able but illiterate predecessors of two thousand and more years ago.

An upland landscape like this may look dull perceived merely as scenery. Yet, while its structure is natural, its appearance is largely an artefact produced by man's activities over some 5000 years. Domesticated animals have prevented regeneration of post-glacial woodland originally cleared for farming, a process continued still by grazing ponies in stone-walled enclosed fields. Quarrying also occurred here in prehistoric times. Bleak and remote moors, like this one on Mynydd Preseli, Dyfed, are often places that still bear the imprint of early human activity.

A PORTFOLIO FROM PREHISTORY

The prehistoric people of Britain were not all that different from us. Their basic needs were somewhere to live, food, an ability to protect their own interests and those of their society, and some form of spiritual life. The differences compared to us lie in the frameworks within which they tried to meet these needs; and those frameworks obviously embrace the environment, the social context, and available resources and technological skills.

Our illustration here of such themes is limited by both our medium and the subjects of the photography. It is difficult to photograph vanished environments, social context, and religious belief; and, in concentrating on what visible remains survive in the present landscape, we are excluding not only whole areas of human experience but also whole fields of evidence about prehistoric man and his activities. The extant but generally invisible remains below ground, the ever expanding contents of museums, and the analytical data derived from microscopic and other scientific examination of many different sorts of prehistoric material are just three sources of evidence which we are not illustrating.

Photography is nonetheless extremely good at portraying the results of human activity where this has produced buildings and earthworks or moulded the landscape through agriculture. It is good at illustrating structural change and succession, hinting at the processes of change even where it cannot explore the social dynamics that lie behind the physical evidence. And, it is good, too, at revealing both geographical context and structural detail.

With these emphases, and knowing them to be biases within the wider study of prehistory, we have arranged the following plates in broad categories to cover four of Man's main needs and activities. Such an arrangement is the product of a modern mind and need bear no relation to how prehistoric people thought about their activities. Nevertheless, we can be sure that they lived, worked, defended themselves and acted out religious beliefs, even while suspecting that such activities were much more closely intertwined than in modern life.

Over the seven or eight thousand years between the early, post-glacial warming of prehistoric Britain and the Roman conquest, people inhabited much of the landscape that we walk and drive through today. Their numbers were, of course, small at first but it would be a mistake to underestimate the population. By the first century BC, two million could well be a conservative estimate.

Relatively few habitation sites were occupied for very long which is why archaeology, almost by definition, is so concerned with the discovery and investigation of *deserted* settlements. In a sense we are nearly always looking at failures, sites which for one reason or another – probably a whole set of reasons – proved unsuitable. Many places were, however, briefly occupied many times over, perhaps seasonally, as part of a chosen way of life. The practice of transhumance, involving at its simplest a shift each spring from a home settlement to a summer habitation and then a return in the autumn, is the best-known of such life-ways; but more complex living-cycles are known or can be inferred, for example among pre-farming communities dependent on the seasonal movements of the animals and fish on which their food supply depended.

During the course of these millennia, then, groups of people ranging from small hunter-bands to incipient urban communities lived in hundreds of thousands of different places in the British landscape. Their settlements ranged from overnight campsites to major, permanent centres enduring for centuries and provided with massive, capital-intensive features such as elaborate defences and prestigious, carved and painted wooden gateways. People lived along river valleys, on coastal plains and beside estuary and sea, around lakes, and on hillsides, the uplands and hilltops. They had the need at one time or another, and the capacity for much of the time, to live almost anywhere. A few remote places were always unsettled and, at any one time, some areas were not available or were deliberately eschewed. Previously habitable places could become flooded, agricultural change might dictate the avoidance of certain types of soil, or political considerations might create areas which were out of bounds.

People lived in and used both natural and man-made shelters. Caves were obvious natural places to occupy. Though their niche in popular imagination is as the home of primitive, skin-clad savages, they were in fact used as living and storage places, and for burial and ceremonial purposes, throughout the 4000 years our photographs cover. It was, how-

Gop Hill cave, Clwyd, at the east end, looking north east. Typical of many caves in Britain, this was used here around the entrance more as a rock-shelter than as a cave proper. It was favoured by animals and then sporadically, over perhaps four thousand years, by man both as living quarters and burial place. Archaeological finds include Pleistocene animal bones, Mesolithic flints including tools and waste flakes, Neolithic burials, pottery, flints and a polished stone axehead, and stone tools probably of second millennium BC date.

ever, only when communities started to build permanent structures using stone in the later fourth millennium BC that they began to create potential ruins that can effectively be recorded using photography. Many buildings were, of course, constructed of wood, earth and thatch and the superstructure of these has everywhere disappeared; but from *c* 3500–3000 BC, the earliest surviving stone-based living structures enable us to begin to appreciate at least some aspects of domestic life among Britain's early farming communities.

Archaeology's acquisition of methods to obtain estimates of absolute date, rather than discoveries of new sites, has transformed this appreciation. Several settlement complexes in the Orkneys and Shetlands, for example, long known and recognised as 'early', have now been back-dated through carbon-14 measurement by one to two thousand years. Britain still lacks, however, at least in bulk, the ground plans of serried ranks of large rectangular and trapezoidal, post-built wooden halls familiar in continental north-west Europe as the homes of early farmers.

From the last three millennia BC, surviving stone ruins, supplemented by much excavated evidence of timber buildings from the English lowlands and from beneath stone foundations in the uplands, provide us with a range of settlement types and buildings. The bulk and diversity of this evidence is considerable, and its spread over time can be interpreted in a number of different, and not necessarily compatible, ways. Round buildings became the norm during the 2nd and 1st millennia, with stone footings, even walls, in the uplands, and a variety of timber construction methods in stoneless areas. So strong was the timber tradition in later prehistoric times that, for example, on the Marlborough Downs and Cheviot where stone was available, buildings were still entirely of wood. All over the landscape, round buildings occurred in a range of sizes presumably reflecting both status and function, and in settlements ranging from farmsteads to conglomerations bespeaking hundreds of inhabitants. Especially was this so in some of the large hill-forts of the last centuries BC.

Perhaps the most significant fact, however, is simply that Britain possesses an extensive and varied heritage vividly illustrating how our ancestors lived two thousand and more years ago. The actual evidence, surviving on and in the ground, is a reservoir of great but as yet unassessable knowledge and its quality makes it of far more than merely national significance.

This view of House I at the Neolithic village of Skara Brae on Orkney Mainland looks towards the entrance in use during the first centuries of the third millennium BC. Living quarters of the people of this period are rare anywhere, and here we not only have a whole cluster of houses but houses complete with their original fittings and furniture. This is the result of excellent preservation by wind-blown sand and the ready availability of local sandstone which splits off the natural rock in flat, rectilinear slabs – rather like sheets of blockboard from today's DIY superstore. Here we see, in detail unequalled for most of prehistory, the box-beds and cupboards around the walls of a four-thousand-year-old, all-purpose living room. In the centre is a large fireplace and, near it, items of stone equipment and a small tank for water or possibly fresh fish or bait.

Settlements and houses, including those of the earliest farming communities, also survive well on the Shetland Isles. This particular Neolithic settlement is at Scord of Brouster, West Mainland, located at the head of Gruting Voe and here seen looking south-east. The site as a whole covers at least 2.5 hectares. It consists of six contiguous, irregularly shaped, stone-divided enclosures in a cluster. Within them are numerous mounds of stones cleared off the land for farming, a kerbed cairn, and three houses. House 1, 7 m by 5 m internally with its entrance downslope at the gable-end, and the much later (perhaps third century AD) kerb cairn, were both excavated in the 1970s; they lie in the foreground here, with the remains of field-walls just visible round about. Similar evidence exists along the western side of the Voe (to the right of the photograph), providing an excellent indication of where and how people lived and worked in 'a locally well-filled landscape', to use Alasdair Whittle's vivid phrase, in the centuries either side of 2000 BC.

Stanydale on West Mainland is another Shetland Neolithic settlement. It consists of four substantial houses, oval in plan, set in a complex of field-walls and clearance cairns like that at Scord of Brouster. Visible here are the excavated remains of one of the characteristic smaller houses, looking south-east over the rear wall, the porched entrance lying downslope at the far end. Internal fittings include a hearth, wall-bench and wall-cupboards, features similar to those in the broadly contemporary houses of Neolithic Orkney. Typical of Shetland, this house was built and occupied by farmers in the centuries towards 2000 BC.

The Stanydale 'temple', the largest building on the site, looking west along its length from the entrance down a passage set in the thickness of the walls. The internal sill-stone marks the place where a wooden inner door was once hung or slotted. On line with the passage are two stone-packed holes in the floor, representing part of a vanished timber superstructure. An upright wooden post in each would have supported the ridge-pole at the apex of the roof. Preserved fragments of one of the posts have proved on examination to be spruce, a tree unknown in Shetland at the time and likely therefore to have reached the island as driftwood from across the North Atlantic. The further half of the oval interior has six recesses in the wall, hinting perhaps that this structure was a temple or chieftain's hall rather than a mere house.

Neolithic settlements are not confined to Shetland Mainland. This further example is on the island of Whalsay off the east coast. The site itself lies on a slope to the east, overlooking Yoxie Geo. Known as Pettigarths Field, it consists of a tomb and two houses, one rather confusingly called the 'Standing Stones of Yoxie' and the other the 'Benie Hoose' or 'Bunzie House'. Here we are looking south-south-east over the back wall of the latter, the entrance into its adjoining yard on the left. The site was prepared by cutting back into the natural rock to make a level platform. When excavated archaeologically some four thousand years later, the structure produced nearly 2000 stone implements, principally discs, grain-rubbing stones, hammerstones and pounders. This may be the debris of normal domesticity over a long period but other possibilities for the use of the building include store-place or workshop. Perhaps such functions were simultaneous and not distinguished by the inhabitants.

Almost at the other end of Britain on Rough Tor, Bodmin Moor, Cornwall, a similar continuum of living, working and believing can be inferred. Looking south from the Tor, beyond the scree in the immediate foreground, we survey a landscape now superficially barren, even desolate, but one that was intensively used in the second millennium BC. Remains of settlements with stone foundations of round houses prove people lived here, while field systems, visible as lines of stones, show that they were farming. In the middle distance lies a stone circle in the full, ceremonial sense. It is called Fernacre.

Dartmoor too is a landscape of great antiquity and numerous antiquities. Much of it was extensively utilised in the second millennium BC as the widespread evidence of farms and field systems, burial mounds and ceremonial sites illustrate. At Kes Tor the minor road from Chagford up to Batworthy actually bends round one of the settlements on its south-eastern side, here the point of view. The site is not an isolated one but part of an impressively organised rectilinear land allotment system of the mid-second millennium BC. The divisions are still marked on the ground by banked lines of stone and earth known as reaves. These delimit blocks of land and their internal boundaries around fields, farms and contemporary tracks. The site here is in fact one of several settlements in the area, each containing several round houses and each fitting into the 'organised landscape' of three and a half thousand years ago. This particular settlement has been excavated, producing evidence of occupation into the first millennium BC. Slag from ironworking was also found.

At the Merrivale settlement, today conveniently placed for visits on either side of the B3357 road across Dartmoor, numerous pounds, houses and farm buildings of the second millennium BC can readily be seen. Here, lying a few metres south of the modern road, is one 'hut circle': the stone foundations and ruinous wall of a round building, probably a house, the tumbled remains of what was probably the doorway lying nearest the camera. It is part of an extensive settlement which contains small enclosures but appears not to have been surrounded by an enclosing wall overall. A short distance south lie two stone rows, a stone circle and a standing stone. One of the boundaries of the reave system passes to its west.

Though it retains a less obvious 'prehistoric' character, this landscape too was settled and farmed in the second and first millennia BC; indeed traces of still earlier settlement survive to show that this is a man-made landscape of very great age. In contrast to the now marginal moors of Shetland, Bodmin and Dartmoor, however, here farming continues, largely for arable crops and on an intensive scale. Berwick Down near Tollard Royal in Wiltshire, seen here looking south from beside the South Wiltshire Ridgeway, is a long spur of chalk running towards and beyond the north end of the belt of trees in the middle distance. Along it lie three settlements, probably successive one to the other, running through the second half of the first millennium BC and into the Roman period. The earliest is at the nearer end on the higher ground by the nearest tree-clump: it was unenclosed, consisting only of a few round timber buildings and pits for corn storage. At the lower end of the spur stood a small enclosed farmstead, excavated and now ploughed flat, occupied in a late phase of the Iron Age around the time of the birth of Christ. Surrounding fields doubtless produced the grain we know to have been stored in wooden granaries beside its round timber house. Between, lying just left of centre in the grassland, lay the third and latest settlement. Almost certainly originating in pre-Roman times, it developed in its later stages into a characteristic Romano-British enclosed farmstead. To have three sequential prehistoric settlements laid out side by side like this, rather than superimposed, is rare.

(Opposite page) While Ardanaiseig crannog in Loch Awe, Argyll, looks wholly different from Berwick Down, the two sites were actually inhabited at the same time, in the last centuries BC. Probably each group of inhabitants had a water problem too – though at either end of the range of such problems. Water collection and storage on the porous chalk Downs of Wessex was always a difficulty whereas it was the very abundance of water at Loch Awe which made the place attractive for living, even while it impeded access. Around the shores, in particular, some security could be gained relatively easily by building a small artifical island of logs, planks, piles and stones, and then living on it in a timber house. Access was by boat or, sometimes, a narrow causeway linking crannog and shore. The organic density of these structures means that nowadays they are often marked, as here, by naturally seeded clumps of trees.

High on the southern edge of the Cheviot massif in Northumberland are two adjacent enclosed settlements at High Knowes, Alnham. One, containing four round timber buildings, was surrounded by a double palisade. The narrow trenches for its timber posts are still clearly visible, reflected in genuinely old grassland by lines of more verdant fescue among the prevailing nardus. Nothing seems to have disturbed the foreground area of the photograph over the two thousand years since the posts were removed or rotted in the last centuries BC.

(Opposite page) Milton Loch crannog in Dumfries and Galloway is one of the best explored of these man-made islets. The tops of the two wooden posts sticking out of the water to the left of the crannog represent a substructure of many piles originally supporting a planked causeway to the shore. Timber piling around the islet consolidates the foundations so that the house floor would have stood just above water level. On the loch side of the crannog, right, further timber and stonework was used to construct a small harbour.

The structures in which people lived in the last centuries BC varied greatly in form – as do the local names for them now. Where the hand of Roman was light or non-existent, buildings often continued to be occupied into the early centuries AD. The Wag of Forse, near Latheron in Caithness, illustrates these points well. This photograph is of one of the houses there, part of the later phases of a complex settlement. It is rectangular, 12 m long, apparently with two stone rows inside it. These are remnants of what appears to have been a curious way of supporting the roof. As the arrangement in the right foreground shows, lintels lay between pillar-top and wall so at the very least there would originally have been low, covered areas down each side of the interior.

(Below right) Another distinctive type of late prehistoric living place is the 'wheel-house', characterised here by an example from Jarlshof, Shetland. The name refers to the appearance of the house in plan where piers projecting inwards from the circular perimeter wall look a bit like the spokes of a wheel. We could be seeing a skeuomorph, a fabrication in stone of the framework and interior of a timber house, prehistoric in terms of its cultural situation but in date probably belonging to the early centuries AD. Each of the drystone piers features a basal facing stone, dividing the outer zone of the floor into a series of compartments, perhaps for storage, even a little privacy.

(Above) At the other end of Britain, Carn Euny courtyard-house village near Sancreed and Land's End, Cornwall, gives a good impression of the structural complexity still discernible within a settlement built in stone and occupied for perhaps a thousand years either side of 1 AD. One of its main attractions is an underground structure called a 'fogou', a characteristic feature of late prehistoric sites in Cornwall. Here we look north-north-west, uphill at most of the village with one of the houses in the foreground. People were living in this at the same time as others were living in wags, wheel-houses and crannogs 600 miles to the north.

This site in Sutherland at Kilphedir in the Strath of Kildonan is a settlement area rather than a discrete site like Carn Euny. Though partly excavated, most of the elements shown here survive in a manner typical of prehistoric settlements throughout upland Britain. As at Carn Euny, the settlement contains an underground chamber, here called a 'souterrain' rather than a fogou. Its entrance, beneath the wall nearest to the camera, is from the interior of the ruins (in the foreground) of the largest of three scattered round houses and leads into an underground passage c 9.50 m long, mostly outside the circle of the house wall. Nearby are other buildings and a ruined broch.

(Below left) At Ardestie near Dundee a comparable souterrain has been fully excavated, a report published, and the remains consolidated for display to the public. Here we look north-east with the relationship between the souterrain or underground chamber and the 'rooms' of the building above clearly visible. The price to be paid for this clarity, however, is that no good impression can be gained of what it was actually like inside a souterrain. The lintelled roof and overburden of earth have been removed for display purposes.

(Above) An example of extensive late prehistoric settlement in a strikingly different landscape is Crosby Garret near Newbiggin on Lune in Cumbria. In the form of grass-covered earthworks rather than bare stone ruins, three villages lie among fields and tracks covering at least 65 hectares. Here, at the largest settlement, the approach road, now looking like a silted-up ditch, leads south-east towards a series of enclosures, paddocks, garden plots and houses. Such features can be seen in relief but their 'humpiness' is accentuated by shorter dark grass against a general background of long bleached stalks.

North Wales is another area where numerous late prehistoric settlements survive. Among the several archaeological sites open to the public on Anglesey, two such settlements are well preserved and easily accessible. Ty Mawr is on Holyhead Mountain, apparently a village of round houses scattered on a slope above a cliff-top plateau which would have provided relatively good agricultural land or pasture. On its east side, however, is a larger, compact unit, that has recently been excavated. It appears to be one farm-cum-family steading, consisting of two round buildings and a yard contained within an oval enclosure, here seen looking east. Occupation certainly began before the Roman conquest of Anglesey and the site in this form belongs to the last centuries BC. Its inhabitants cultivated cereals in fields nearby and collected limpets along the sea-shore.

Din Lligwy, also on Anglesey, is one of the most impressive-looking small settlements in Britain. It is also typical of another variety of late prehistoric occupation site in North Wales, consisting of a rectilinear stone-walled enclosure which contains several buildings and space for a yard. Here we look south-east from the enclosure wall with circular buildings visible in the foreground and to the rear with rectangular structures to the right. The entrance is to the rear left and most of the central area is open. The whole site has an air of being intended to impress, as if occupied by the family of a reasonably well-to-do farmer, a local man who nevertheless knew, perhaps at second hand, about the country villas in the distant south lived in by people such as he aspired to be. For, although it originated before the Conquest, this residence as we see it is essentially of the Roman period.

Working

Prehistoric people worked above all with their hands. The human body was the common machine in the millennia before mechanisation, and the workers of prehistory were involved in manual labour and concerned with materials to an extent that is alien to common experience in western societies today.

To stress this is in no way to demean the mental abilities of prehistoric people, not least because much of their material culture can be interpreted in terms of a long and successful quest to improve the technologies available to them. In modern terms these people were clearly first-class field geologists-cum-naturalists who sought, found and exploited many of the natural resources of the British landscape. The use of flint and igneous rocks and then metal-bearing ores to meet the need for edged tools, weapons and prestige objects is an outstanding example of this drive and skill. The urge not only to make tasks easier but also to make their execution more efficient was quite as strong in 2000 BC as in the later twentieth century AD.

It would be wrong also to think of prehistoric time as a long period in which not much happened. It is the last three centuries, our immediate and familiar background, which are so exceptional, in a world perspective and through time, in their *pace* of change, especially when it comes to new inventions and their technological application. On a longer time-scale, developments were adopted more slowly and seem to have come in less of a spate. Nevertheless, during the four millennia that concern us here profound changes took place, and some underpin our working lives still.

Farming developed as the basis of life in Britain during the fourth millennium BC so most manual work thereafter can be seen as stemming directly or indirectly from domesticated food production. That, of course, involves animals and grass, woodland, birds and fish, as much as cereal, pulse and vegetable cultivation. It is not difficult to envisage how most people spent most of their time, for pre-mechanical agriculture in the widest sense of crop production is well known to be time-consuming and labour intensive. And that is true long before a community arrives at a situation in which it controls and is effectively managing its crop and stock, its fields and woodland, and its water supply. All such resources have to be worked for, and primarily that means clearing rough land of trees, bushes and stones. Chopping and hauling must have been familiar tasks, unphotographable now but clearly evidenced by the remnant landscapes of the third millennium, the planned landscapes of the second millennium fossilised on the uplands, and the extensive lowland landscapes of the first millennium revealed in our own time by aerial photography. And such activities were still 'work', in the sense that they required the expenditure of human energy, even when the purpose was less mundane and aimed at higher aspirations of the mind and soul in the form of megalithic tombs; henge monuments and stone circles. Whether prehistoric workers made the distinction we do between the pragmatic and the spiritual may well be doubted.

All this labour was, of course, aided by tools, animals and simple technology. The wheel was known from c 2000 BC though we have no certain evidence of its application other than to pottery making until late in British prehistory. The basic tool-kit of the arable farmer was available, variously in wood, leather, stone, flint, bronze and eventually iron, from the later fourth millennium. A relatively simple but effective type of plough was available from before 3000 BC, doubtless complemented by a range of different implements for the multifarious tasks involved in preparing the ground for crop production on a variety of soils. Horses were bred but oxen provided the single most significant source of energy for human needs. It is probably only a slight exaggeration to say that the crop-based economy of later prehistoric Britain depended on them. A great deal of work, therefore, would have been taken up in breeding, looking after, and training oxen. The prehistoric pace of life accordingly was perhaps two miles per hour, the natural speed of a well-trained and willing ox.

Many aspects of prehistoric work are not too difficult to envisage and are experienced still by all those agricultural communities around the world dependent on technologically simple, labour-intensive food production; but the labour and daily reality are quite beyond the experience of most people in Britain and America today. Three elements therefore need to be emphasised. First, to a degree we find difficult to appreciate, wood was *the* material which was daily in the hands of prehistoric people, finding and fetching it, growing it to required strengths and dimensions, shaping it, using it. Second, much daily work was skilled, requiring considerable knowledge, planning, and strategic decision-making about matters such as changes in land-use. At an individual level, much of it also involved what we would now call crafts, especially in carpentry, potting, masonry, metal-working and jewellery. Third, much of the work we see attested in the structures in this book involved considerable organisation and communal effort, clearly implying the availability of a large labour force and the existence in the background of unifying forces stemming from strong cultural tradition and the exercise of political and religious power. If only we knew how any one of these actually worked.

We can see, in short, what prehistoric people did and often infer with some certainty how they did it; but precise explanations of why they worked as they did remain very difficult to formulate.

Pike of Stickle, Great Langdale, Cumbria, looking east — one of several areas in the Lake District where stone was quarried and roughly shaped for tool-making during the third millennium BC before being transported for finishing elsewhere. Here greenstone was worked from the outcrops at the top, with the result that the slopes below are strewn with waste. The products of this axe factory have been recovered in contemporary contexts over much of England, the densest concentrations in Lancashire and across the Pennines in the Trent and Humber Basins.

(Overleaf) Another area of early quarrying was on the Carn Meini dolerite outcrop in the Preseli Hills, Dyfed, South Wales, the area from which the blue-stones at Stonehenge were extracted round about 2000 BC. The distribution of stone axes from this source was, however, more restricted, extending only as far east as the Severn Valley. In this view we are looking south-south-west from the central cairn of three inside the innermost enclosure of Foel (or Moel) Trigarn hillfort, named in Welsh after the existence of the cairns. The blue-stone outcrop lies behind to the left. Recent field survey has also revealed evidence of prehistoric settlement and farming in the area.

The most accessible of Britain's Neolithic flint-mines is Grimes Graves on the Breckland near Brandon in Norfolk, where numbers of shafts have been excavated and one mine is open to the public. The complex is of almost Industrial Revolution proportions: 14 hectares containing upwards of 360 shafts and quarries as much as 9 m deep, with many lengths of gallery radiating from the bottom of the deeper shafts. This is one such gallery (not open to the public) in Canon Greenwell's Pit, so named after its Victorian excavator, looking towards the seam of flint which was the miners' target. Flint nodules have evidently been prised from the holes in the pitted chalk floor.

At the bottom of the same pit, looking south at the undisturbed end of a gallery where it seems work has just stopped. The seam is of good quality flint, the antler picks are ready for work; flint nodules and chalk debris wait in vain to be removed. Why did the miners never come back?

(Above) This small, local Neolithic quarry is an example of many that doubtless still remain to be discovered. It is on North Roe, Shetland, at the Beorgs of Uyea, where a large outcrop of blue-grey felsite has been quarried. The resulting pit has been covered with horizontal slabs to produce what is in effect the entrance to a mine, surrounded by the debris from quarrying and roughing out a range of tools. The felsite was used to make axes and also polished oval knives and other implements, apparently only for local use.

The chalklands of southern England do not possess the hard, metamorphic rocks of the west and north exploited by the early farming communities of Britain for so much of their equipment in the third and early second millennia BC. The Neolithic inhabitants of the south therefore turned, as their predecessors had for millennia, to the flint that was locally available. The difference was that, from c 3000 BC, they quarried it. At Cissbury, West Sussex, inside the very much later hillfort, depressions such as this one are the tops of flint-mine shafts four to five thousand years old.

The prehistoric working of metal is visually much more difficult to illustrate than that of stone, the main archaeological evidences being smelting hearths or hoards of scrap-metal, generally bronze. But here, in House III at Jarlshof, Shetland, is one of the many examples where excavation has revealed a building structurally like any other that was used as a metalworking shop, in this case as early as c 800 BC. Already an abandoned ruin, the remains of its several small rooms were doubtless convenient for the production of bronze swords, axes and other objects, the broken clay moulds for which survived together with traces of the smithy. Opinions differ as to whether the bronze-worker who operated here was an itinerant smith from Ireland or the retainer of a local warlord.

The collection and shaping of timber was an almost daily task in prehistoric Britain, but the population's involvement with wood as a material goes much deeper than this. From Neolithic times, woodland was managed to produce timber in various forms for a whole range of different purposes. While we can find the products of this long-term management, for example in the waterlogged prehistoric trackways of the Somerset Levels, we cannot photograph a live prehistoric wood in a managed state. Nevertheless, woodland scenes like this must have been commonplace throughout prehistoric Britain: cut and stacked hazel wands with regenerating hazel under a broken canopy of mature oaks, seen here at Rushbeds Wood Nature Reserve, near Brill, Buckinghamshire.

(Above) Rushbeds Wood also illustrates the farming practice of coppicing, common in much of the English countryside until quite recently and known for certain to have been followed in prehistoric times. These coppiced hazel stools, ready for cutting, offer stems suitable for fencing, wattling, basketry and firewood. Prehistoric people observed from childhood what every forester and estate-manager knows still to be the case, that timber is a crop just like cabbages and cereals, the only difference being that its cropping-cycle is somewhat longer.

No complete wooden house survives from prehistory so we turn to modern replication and experiment to illustrate timber in use as it could have been c 300 BC. This is one of several possible reconstructions of a house excavated at foundation level at Moel y Gaer in North Wales, erected on part of the Demonstration Area at Butser Ancient Farm near Petersfield, Hampshire. In this unfinished state, the skeleton of the structure vividly illustrates the dependence on organic materials — here principally wood, straw and daub — of prehistoric man in lowland Britain in contrast to the uplands where stone was always readily available. Yet even organic materials needed to be won: to produce the timber alone required forethought and management over years so that the right woods, from the appropriate trees and of the correct lengths, thicknesses and strengths, were ready for cropping at the right time.

(Below) Land cleared was divided, for crop rotation, for separating arable from pasture, for demarcating territory and property. On softer subsoils like gravel and, as here, chalk, long boundary ditches were dug across the landscape, the spoil from them being thrown to one or both sides. This typical example, probably of the second millennium BC, is several kilometres long and part of a system of land division on the Marlborough Downs in Wiltshire. It lies across the line of The Ridgeway below Adam's Grave, just north of Knap Hill and overlooking the Vale of Pewsey.

From c 4000 BC onwards, the cropping of cereals and breeding of domestic animals for food came to dominate day to day work. All over Britain land had to be cleared: a colossal task, fundamental to the appearance of the landscape around us today. Archaeologically, however, the common structural survival of this long-drawn-out process is slight and undramatic: heaps of stones rather grandly called cairns. Often occurring in cairn-fields of dozens, even hundreds, they bear witness in this case to clearance for prehistoric farming at Danby Rigg on the North Yorkshire Moors. Tens of thousands of similar cairns survive in Britain's stony uplands. They were not, of course, built to be monumental; but, en masse, they are genuinely a monument to the achievement by prehistoric Britons of perhaps their single greatest task, the establishment of a way of life based on successful crop production.

(Left) Enclosed land with its boundary bank from the age of agricultural improvement in the eighteenth/nineteenth centuries AD contrasts with the apparently unimproved moorland beyond. Yet the moorland is in fact the derelict landscape of enclosures cleared and farmed in the second millennium BC. This north-facing slope is dotted with a series of stone-walled enclosures, either farmsteads or animal pounds, and divided by long, low walls. Presumably its farmers cropped the nearer slope too but the later improvements there have removed the evidence. Here we are looking at the north side of Rough Tor on the northern edge of Bodmin Moor, Cornwall. This sort of landscape, with its ebb and flow of land use on the margin of cultivable land, is replicated throughout upland Britain.

(Left) Walls of prehistoric fields survive not only on moorland but also beneath peat. Peat-formation may have been one of several reasons for the abandonment of upland areas by farmers all over the British Isles in the centuries either side of 1000 BC. Gently accumulating against and then over walls, the peat has in effect cocooned them for perhaps three thousand years. Now, where peat-digging is continued in the traditional way by hand, we can study in detail the handiwork of farmers who laid out their fields in a more varied natural environment than today's. This example is at Nuckro Water, Whalsay, Shetland.

(Below) The land had to be cultivated to grow crops. Cultivation, whether with a spade or early form of plough, disturbs the ground in ways which are still sometimes detectable. Some of the best evidence comes in the form of slight ridges and furrows which have survived since the first millennium BC on the surface of land which has sub-sequently not been much disturbed. One of many such examples is near Greenlee Lough in Northumberland, just north of Hadrian's Wall, here forming the skyline in the photograph. The undulations in the foreground are man-made, less than a metre wide and only a few centimetres high; yet they are quite certainly the result of cultiv-ation and pre-Roman in date. They are part of an extensive area of such cultivation remains, both inside and outside a Roman camp, the bank and ditch of which cuts across them, showing them to be earlier.

(Above) This stone wall between ancient fields in the Maen-y-Bardd area, North Wales, contains a very rare detail. The line of the downhill wall-face is interrupted by a break and, behind the gap, a metre or so uphill, is a short length of wall or revetment holding back the soil. On either side of it are ramps leading down from the higher field to the lower. With a little imagination, we can almost see the prehistoric farmer, not ploughing or digging this time but carrying his implements shoulder-high from one ploughed field to another or coaxing his stock through a narrow gap, normally closed with a bit of hurdling, from one grazed field to a fresh paddock.

51

On East Moor, Bodmin Moor, Cornwall, is another vivid surviving detail of everyday prehistoric life. The pair of standing stones, at first glance upright in isolation, fit into a familiar pattern of second millennium fields. Low, collapsed walls run left from the left-hand stone of the pair, and right from the right-hand one; but not between them. They form, in other words, a gateway, not in itself remarkable except that it is some 3000 years old. Probably it was closed by a woven hurdle or other timber and not a hinged gate and was intended to control cattle rather than sheep (which would jump it). It is only 1.07 m wide, like the passage between the fields in the previous photograph, and was therefore most probably for foot traffic, man and beast, rather than wheeled vehicles.

The best evidence for the preparation of food comes as waste products, often in middens, and in the form of stones used in rubbing, grinding and pounding. The stone equipment often seems cumbersome, requiring a lot of elbow grease to operate. Here, lying on the floor of a prehistoric house at Jarlshof, Shetland, are two boulder or trough querns. Their basin-like appearance is largely the result of many years' wear for raw materials have evidently been bashed, mashed and smashed by the two-handed pounder-stones in ever-deepening depressions. These particular examples may have been discarded, the right-hand end of each being worn through.

Another sort of prehistoric mound more significant than its appearance suggests is very much connected with the preparation of food. In the foreground here at Cefn Trefor-isaf, Bryncir, near Porthmadog, Gwynedd, is one example; another is in the middle distance in front of the nearest tree, and three others lie in the area. These mounds consist of the debris from prehistoric cooking, repeated many times in the same place around open-air hearths. An alternative technique was to cook food not over an open fire but in containers full of water heated by dropping in hot stones.

Fish and shell-fish could well have been cooked in heated water-tanks. This detail is of a (reconstructed) kitchen midden in the Bronze Age area at Jarlshof, Shetland. With its many limpet shells in a matrix of myriad shell fragments, it exemplifies food refuse characteristic of prehistoric coastal settlements and, where they were powerful or rich, inland ones too.

Prehistoric routes and trackways are difficult to identify with certainty in the modern landscape but one with better credentials than most is the Icknield Way in Oxfordshire, Buckinghamshire and Hertfordshire. As a through-route, it may have begun on Salisbury Plain, even at Stonehenge, following the crest of the Marlborough Downs as the present-day Ridgeway to the Goring Gap on the River Thames. As the Icknield Way it then strikes north-east along the foot of the Chiltern Hills towards East Anglia. While its general line is probably that of a prehistoric route, any particular stretch must necessarily be regarded with suspicion as a genuine length of prehistoric road. Here we look north-east along the Upper Icknield Way near Princes Risborough, Buckinghamshire. Though the track here is unmetalled and feels appropriately ancient with its high, unkempt hedges tangled in Old Man's Beard and honeysuckle, just round the corner it becomes a tarmacadamed road.

An upland version of a prehistoric route, also marked by a still-used track, is the Ffordd Ddu trackway near Barmouth, Gwynedd. Here it is seen heading north-north-east towards Snowdonia as it skirts the north side of Cader Idris between Llwyngwril and Dolgellau. Part of it became the Roman road from Brithdir to Pennal. On the left is the earthwork of a Romano-British enclosure.

Uncertain as are the lines of prehistoric routes, even more dubious are the claims to great antiquity of bridges and fords. Britain does not now possess an identifiable prehistoric bridge, it seeming likely that such as existed were in timber rather than stone. The best generic claimant in stone is the clapper bridge, a type of megalithic structure occurring in parts of Devon and Cornwall, and here exemplified by one at Bellever near Postbridge on Dartmoor. Even if the type originates in prehistoric times, which is doubtful, none of the surviving examples is unfortunately likely to be older than medieval at best.

Defending

One of the enduring myths of prehistory is that people, blissfully unaware of what was coming in the way of trouble and strife, lived in continuously peaceful accord with Nature and each other. We want to believe this, of course, as the recently exposed hoax of a supposedly Neolithic tribe in Papua New Guinea has so sadly shown, but there is no more reason to believe it true of prehistoric Britons than of the late-twentieth-century population. However regrettably, our forebears have left us plentiful evidence of their discord, and to such an extent that our problem is not to argue whether or not they fought but to discover how they fought and what their fighting was about.

It has been something of a shock to interpreters of the British archaeological record to discover that such is the case. It has been known for years that flint-tipped arrows were very much part of early farmers' equipment. Nevertheless, partly because of the lack of defensive earthworks in the Neolithic landscape and of obviously offensive weaponry in their tool-kit, partly because people obviously needed arrows to shoot animals and birds and, it has to be admitted, partly because of the silent influence of the 'noble savage', it was for long assumed that early farming communities did not fight each other. Why should they? They were few in number, there was plenty of room and no occasion for tension. Yet now, from recent fieldwork and excavations, notably at Carn Brea, Cornwall, Hambledon Hill, Dorset, and Crickley Hill, Gloucestershire, we have Neolithic hillforts and defences, fortified entrances, and, from the last-named site, clear evidence of a final assault in which Neolithic bowmen shot their flint-tipped arrows at opposing forces defending the ramparts and gateways.

In fact, the really new element here is the early date, round about 2500 BC. Without wishing to give the impression that warfare was endemic throughout prehistory, evidence for defence and fighting is unquestionably common.

In broad terms, the militaristic element in prehistoric affairs appears to increase through the second millennium – though this may be partly because specifically fighting equipment, such as swords, was made and, being metal, survives to figure prominently in the archaeological record. For the earlier part of that millennium too, British society was following the archaeologically useful fashion of individual inhumation burial with accompanying grave-goods. Quite a lot of military-looking equipment has thus survived and been found in excavation.

It is clearly unsafe, however, to construct inferences pretending to great authority on a basis of evidence which is clearly biased in several ways. There may or may not have been armies, military affairs and aggressive intents in later prehistoric Britain but the main thrust of the field evidence is defence, and static defence at that. Further, the intent of much defence work may well have been protective, against animals as well as humans, rather than militarily defensive; some of it seems to have been primarily a chiefly status symbol, perhaps even just for show and not functionally defensive at all. On the other hand, at the end of prehistory in southern England, we have good documentary evidence for the Roman army militarily assaulting a number of British hillforts and dramatic evidence from Maiden Castle and Hod Hill, both in Dorset, that they were two of them. Both fell. All the way down through the settlement scale of the first millennium BC from such large forts – which in some respects were the local equivalent of walled medieval towns – to individual homesteads, we see the evidence of the desire, even perhaps the genuine need, to enclose living areas. Rampart, bank and ditch, stone wall, palisade: they were all used. And men sought protection in topography too by putting their defences round hilltops, across peninsulae and between converging rivers, and by exploiting natural features such as sheer cliffs, steep slopes and open water. In the last centuries BC there was a sense of insecurity about; there was also, one suspects, some pressure to build material expressions of status in a society which attached considerable importance to display.

This is not the place to develop a discussion on the psychology of belligerence, defence mechanisms and military symbolism, even though all three probably lie close to an understanding of the origins and development of the sites and structures illustrated here. Indeed in some cases, despite appearances, it is difficult to be certain whether 'defending' is the appropriate way of interpreting these monuments. We can be sure, however, that most people throughout the last 4000 years of prehistory had to give considerable thought to their personal safety and, from time to time, put considerable effort into the security of the community too.

Carn Brea, near Redruth in Cornwall, is in several respects typical of many hilltops in Britain. It has been used repeatedly during the last 5000 years, as living-place, for defence, for farming, as a source of minerals and stone, and for open-air meetings. Given its locally dominating position, this is perhaps not surprising. It was lived on and defended around 3000 BC when its slopes were also cultivated. It became a massive, defensive hillfort in the last centuries BC when its interior contained stone-footed round buildings. Despite appearances, the tower is basically genuine, a small medieval 'castle' used for a long time as a hunting lodge and then somewhat over-Gothicised as a Victorian folly. The hilltop was further enhanced in 1836 with a monument to Sir Francis Basset, JP. In this view, looking south-west, the late prehistoric ramparts lie along the hillside to the right.

(Below) Crickley Hill in Gloucestershire is a locally prominent spur jutting forward from the western scarp of the Cotswolds. Here we look west from the modern display platform near the heavily fortified Iron Age entrance. Inside, in the centuries around 500 BC, the foreground was densely occupied with, first, rectangular and, later, round houses. The outlines of some of them are marked by wooden roundels at ground level. Much earlier, c 3000 BC, the end of the spur was defended by ramparts and ditches, still visible in the rough ground in the middle of the photograph. These defences were found on excavation to have been assaulted – arrowheads lay thickly along the former entrance passage-ways through the rampart – and burnt.

(Above right) At Hambledon Hill near Child Okeford in Dorset, looking south at the western ramparts of one of the finest hillforts in Britain, we see the early Iron Age defences enclosing the end of the spur; later the ramparts were extended along the hillside towards the camera and right round the hilltop. Well-preserved building platforms were cut into the slopes. Hambledon was equally an important place in the fourth/third millennia BC with an earthen long barrow (beneath the two bushes on the skyline), a ceremonial centre, a defensive enclosure, dykes across the spurs radiating from the hilltop and probably settlement too. General Wolfe later trained his troops here for the assault on the Heights of Abraham, Quebec, in 1759.

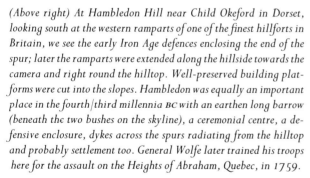

Curiously, given the number of appropriate hilltops, few hillforts were built along the Chilterns. An exception is on Ivinghoe Beacon near Tring, Buckinghamshire, here seen looking south-south-east from Ivinghoe Aston. The position is dramatic for central southern England and a popular viewing point; but there is not much archaeology to see on the ground now. Ironically, the absence of impressive earthworks points to the archaeological significance of the hill: its defences were among the earliest to be built in Britain in the first millennium BC but, timber-built, they decayed without much trace. Unlike so many hillforts, the site was not again defended and, consequently, it did not acquire the multiplicity of earthen ramparts seen, for example, at Hambledon Hill.

(Overleaf) This low-level photograph looking upwards and south-south-west from the Milfield Plain shows the bulk of Yeavering Bell near Kirknewton, Northumberland, the dominant hill protruding from the northern edge of Cheviot. A hillfort defended by a single stone rampart encloses the two peaks, with an earlier and smaller palisaded enclosure around the higher eastern (left-hand) one. The interior contains well-preserved evidence of about 130 round timber buildings. Occupied in the last centuries BC, it was also inhabited in the Roman period and may well have been the local power-base until superseded by the famous British and Anglian fort and royal palace site at its foot in the mid-first millennium AD.

Here, at Herefordshire Beacon on the Malvern Hills, Hereford and Worcester, the familiar notches in the skyline betray the presence of prehistoric defences. They are supplemented at the summit by the profile of a twelfth-century AD castle which lies within the earliest Iron Age ramparts, enclosing some 3 hectares. As at Hambledon, later earthworks were added encircling about 13 hectares over the whole ridge, on which are many hut circles suggesting, if all were houses lived in simultaneously, a considerable population.

(Left) Few hillforts were built in eastern England and very few survive as earthworks. An exception, though not on a hill, is Warham Camp near Wells-next-the-Sea, Norfolk. This general view of its exterior looking north from the bank of the River Stiffkey shows its defences, two banks and ditches, the former up to c 3 m high, the latter roughly flat-bottomed. Part was cut away when the course of the river changed. The small area enclosed, about 1.4 hectares, suggests a defended homestead rather than a major centre, occupied in the first centuries BC/AD and in the Roman period.

Old Oswestry, Shropshire, reveals a classic hillfort profile in this general view looking south-west. Its impressive entrances and multiple defences represent accretions and adaptations over the last centuries BC around a hill originally occupied apparently without defences. Its complex western entrance has a curious arrangement of large tank-like constructions and a c 90 m long embanked passage. Whether the site was actually the precursor of Oswestry, c 1.5 km to its south (left), in anything but the most general sense is a moot point but similar pairings occurring elsewhere, notably at Old and New Sarum (Salisbury) in Wiltshire, provide a possible counterpart.

Mam Tor, Derbyshire, is one of the impressive sights of the Peak District. Here we look northwards towards Edale, part of a superb view which makes the Tor very popular irrespective of its archaeology. In the foreground are the multiple defences of the hillfort enclosing both the hilltop and part of the surrounding slopes on which are the sites of buildings, some earlier than the defences. The eye-catching feature of the hill now is the quasi-megalithic footpath on its south, recently built to counter the erosion caused by visitors.

Uleybury hillfort in Gloucestershire, another fort in a dramatic position, is located in an area rich in archaeological remains. Its defences run round a Cotswold spur just below the rim of a plateau; the photograph is of the three lines of ramparts on the south-west with trees and the footpath marking the two outer ditches. The interior, continuously cropped, is known from air photography to be dense with occupation features. Beyond the main entrance, off the present road, is Hetty Pegler's Tump, a visitable Neolithic chambered tomb, while between the two but now invisible was a major religious and burial complex with a Roman temple sandwiched between earlier and later structures.

(Overleaf) In a landscape of hillforts, Dolebury overlooks the Churchill Gap through the Mendip Hills, now in the County of Avon. Historically though, the site is firmly embedded in the archaeology of Somerset. The foreground here is occupied by the limestone rubble of Dolebury's single northern rampart, probably originally timber-framed, with part of the much-quarried hillfort interior to the left. A much smaller hillfort used to exist on the opposite side of the Gap, and the site of yet another is marked by the tree-clump on Banwell Hill (centre left). The tree-covered higher land on the skyline in the centre of the photograph is Worlebury Hill, an outcrop of carboniferous limestone overlooking the Bristol Channel also bearing a hillfort.

A puzzling feature of hillfort defences, particularly those of limestone, is the phenomenon known as vitrification. This detail of a piece of vitrified walling from the south-east side of the fort at Carradale Point in Kintyre, Argyll, shows material that has been fused into a solid mass by the firing of the original stone and timber. A chemical change has occurred which obviously creates a very solid piece of walling. Was it, however, brought about deliberately or by accident?

(Opposite page) A problem involving the whole landscape is whether hillforts sat in isolation, aloof from the area around them, or served as the nodal point of their surroundings. This view eastwards from the mountains of the Lleyn Peninsula to Snowdonia in North Wales expresses the problem visually. Just right of centre is the large hillfort of Tre'r Ceiri seen from the summit of Yr Eifl. Was it there to protect the lands about or were they there to support it? Perhaps the questions are not mutually exclusive. It is difficult to envisage life in the hillfort not being dependent on the produce of the area it overlooks. But to say as much is to beg another question, at least here in this mountainous area. Was the great hillfort, 450 m above sea-level, occupied all the year round? Perhaps its primary function was as a place of resort if danger threatened families over-summering with their herds and flocks in the uplands.

In its ramparts and gateways, Tre'r Ceiri possesses defensive characteristics suggesting that it was more than a temporary refuge. It displays status, and even military features. This example of a wall-walk behind a parapet, a rare detail to survive, is on the back of the rampart west of the northern gate. The interior is crowded with house sites, ruined more by early excavators than the passage of time, and they seem divisible into two types and two periods. About twenty are circular and pre-Roman but the great majority, about 150, are roughly rectangular or irregular in plan and of Roman date. It is only at this site, in the words of its investigator, 'that the complete plan of a native town of the Roman period (is) exposed to view' — perhaps a rather unexpected judgement to encounter high in Snowdonia.

Another hillfort in North Wales where impressive detail of defensive arrangements survives is Pen-y-Gaer, Llanbedr-y-Cennin. This is situated on the west side of the Conwy Valley not far to the south of our Maen-y-Bardd survey area. Here we see the defences on the south side looking west: three lines of rampart, with the western entrance just visible extreme right. On the open ground outside the outermost bank on the left and also outside the western entrance are areas of small upright stones identified as chevaux-de-frise.

(Left) This view is from outside the western entrance at Pen-y-Gaer, with the outer rampart on the left, looking south-east. In the foreground, the several small upright stones clearly form a man-made feature and are confidently interpreted as a late prehistoric predecessor of medieval chevaux-de-frise. If so, we have to see this hillfort, and at least some others too, as being not only involved in military matters but also defended against cavalry.

Entrances to defended sites were meant to be both effective and impressive though the remains today, even where parts of the original structure were in stone rather than timber, usually leave much to the imagination. At Garrywhin fort near Ulbster, Caithness, large upright slabs mark the northern entrance, here seen from the outside looking south-west. The two stones on the left respectively mark the rear and front faces of the rampart, while the right-hand stone is at the front of the rampart on the far side of the entrance passage. Despite such good preservation of detail, however, it is still not easy to complete the gateway in the mind's eye from this ruin.

(Left) Defence was also necessary for individual homesteads in the last centuries BC, and later still beyond the pax Romana. The dun at Ardifuar, 11 km north-west of Lochgilphead in Mid Argyll, was being lived in during the early centuries AD, being a special type of fortified dwelling with a restricted distribution. Its narrow entrance on the right passes through substantial walls c 3 m thick, still c 3 m high and enclosing a circular area c 20 m in diameter. Cells occur in the thickness of the wall; a low, stone-faced platform runs round two-thirds of the wall interior; the remains of a staircase are visible to the left; and 1.5 m high on the inner wall face is a rare example of a surviving scarcement, indicating that a range of timber buildings formerly stood against it.

(Opposite page) Burgi Geos on Yell is the wonderful name of this 'blockhouse', another example of a local type of defensive work. Confined to Shetland, only three are in situations as dramatic, remote and dangerous as this. We look west along the stone-lined approach to an outer line of defensive stones behind which is a massively constructed entrance with guard-chambers in the thickness of the wall on either side. The wall itself, c 10.5 m long and 4 m thick, cuts off the end of the headland. Beautiful though the position is, as a place to live in it must surely have been a last resort; but perhaps its real purpose, neutrally definable as status-seeking, was machismo image-building.

Dun Grugaig, near Elgol on the island of Skye, is a defensive site which seems to incorporate elements from several types of site. It is in a spectacular situation, a narrow promontory with a sheer drop to the sea, yet it is overlooked from landward; it is small, c 15 m by c 7.5 m, yet its landward wall is 4.6 m thick and galleried; it has a low entrance with a heavy lintel like a broch-tower, yet its shape overall is rectangular; it had a staircase to the upper gallery going up from the inside of the wall, left of the entrance from this viewpoint looking east-south-east.

Dun Ardtreck, near Carbost, also on Skye, here seen looking west towards Ullinish Point and Oronsay, is also perched on a cliff-top. That seems to have been regarded as sufficient protection on the seaward side because the visible wall, still standing some 2 m high, only forms an arc facing inland, enclosing a small D-shaped area of some 130 sq m. The wall contains galleries, and guard-chamber beside the entrance. The earliest dated occupation here is in the mid-first century BC. Perhaps the structure is a prototype for a more sophisticated type of defensive homestead, the broch, which has stone walls built in a fully circular ground plan.

A broch is essentially a defensible drystone tower for living in but it was fairly clearly a status symbol too. Here we see the apparently well-preserved ruins of a broch in Sutherland, rather confusingly called Dun Dornadilla or Dun Dornaigil. The arc of still-standing broch wall is 6.7 m high, impressive but actually held up by a modern buttress. The low, partly blocked, narrow entrance with a characteristically large, triangular lintel is apparently striving for visual effect. Considerable building-up of the ground level had to be undertaken for the foundations on the far side of the tower as the natural slope of the ground drops away to the Strathmore River on the right.

(Overleaf) This broch was built on its own low peninsula projecting from the shore of Loch of Houlland, Esha Ness, on the north-west coast of mainland Shetland, and was being occupied between about 100 BC and AD 300. Its situation is very similar to that of some crannogs. Of three lines of stone walls protecting the approach to the broch over the natural causeway, the widest and innermost is probably original. Another causeway, perhaps man-made, shows just above water-level stretching from land on the left to an island on the right. The broch itself is still c 2 m high but has largely collapsed. Later buildings were constructed in the rubble and the outer walls across the neck of the peninsula may well be related to them.

In striking contrast to Loch of Houlland is the superb inland position of Kilphedir broch near Helmsdale, Sutherland. This broch is clearly visible up and down the valley, the Strath of Kildonan. Here we are looking down it to the west. The structure itself has collapsed but around it are the grass and bracken-covered remains of outer defences with an entrance through them where the ditch ends on the right. The site is part of the wider Kilphedir settlement area.

The best known of all brochs is that at Mousa in Shetland, occupied in the last century or so BC and into the third century AD when its internal arrangements were altered. Its remarkable survival as a tower, however, seems to owe as much to the lack of subsequent settlement alongside, and hence of stone-robbing for later buildings, as to its isolation on a small island off the east coast of Mainland. It still stands slightly more than 13 m high and is c 15 m in diameter at the base; but internally it is only 6 m across.

The great architectural triumph of the original building at Mousa survives: the stair-well with its flight of stone steps mounting from first-floor level to above the original roof-line. This photograph looks down that stair-well eight steps from the top, showing the steps inside the thickness of the broch wall. They were reached originally by a wooden ladder or wooden stairs to the first-floor timber gallery.

(Left) The changes in the internal arrangements at Mousa in what in southern Britain was the later Roman period were not structurally fundamental; but they changed the appearance significantly. A new internal wall-skin included this flight of voids and also masked the entrances to the intra-mural cells and stairway.

(Opposite page) These massive earthworks have been associated with Cassivellaunus, the British leader against Julius Caesar in 54 BC. Called the Devil's Dyke, they lie along a natural valley at Wheathamstead, Hertfordshire. The span between the tops of the banks is 40 m, the depth from them to the ditch bottom in the foreground 12 m. Lesser banks lie to either side, the whole being some 460 m long and originally longer. Similar huge defences lie in Beech Bottom on the north side of St Albans, 8 km to the south. Both occur in an area central to Catuvellaunian territory in the century between Caesar and Claudius.

Looking not unlike a submarine in profile, Clickhimin is one of the classic brochs, consolidated and laid out after excavation for the public to visit. It lies just outside Lerwick, Shetland, on the shore of a freshwater loch now at a lower water level than was the case in the later first millennium BC when the site was in use. Then, it was on a low, small island joined to the shore by a causeway. The stone 'wall' in the foreground is part of a dock; beyond is a stone-revetted landing-stage. That juts out in front of a stone rampart encircling what was originally an islet, immediately inside it an impressive, free-standing 'blockhouse' entrance providing access to the base of a massive broch. This prestigious building complex succeeded an earlier farmstead of the seventh century BC onwards and the islet continued to be used into the middle of the first millennium AD by people living in and around the broch ruins.

At Stanwick in North Yorkshire an extensive complex of large, late prehistoric banks and ditches encloses some 300 hectares. Clearly constructed in different phases, the site was a north British tribal centre at the period of the Roman conquest but its scattered parts survive incompletely. The well-preserved rampart here, with an entrance on the east of the site, was sectioned to the west where, preserved in position, remains a rock-cut ditch in front of a stone-faced rampart. Excavation of the Tofts near Stanwick church is now adding much more information.

It is difficult enough identifying the gods that prehistoric man worshipped, never mind defining his beliefs. It is also difficult just to locate the places where he worshipped. Yet beyond such pressing practical problems are the even more intractable ones of trying to discuss belief in illiterate societies four thousand and more years ago which were living a spiritual life developed from bases totally alien to our own. The only thing we can say for certain about prehistoric belief, and that because the terms of reference are our own, is that it was pagan.

Occasionally, we are given glimpses of what might have been. A wooden 'god dolly', for example, was recently found preserved by waterlogging in the Somerset Levels. It dates to c 3500 BC. It looks like an idol; it might represent 'basic fertility'. But even if such identification is correct, how closely does our concept of that estimable idea correlate with the thoughts and beliefs of an early farmer in Somerset c 5500 years ago? Similarly, but at the other end of our timescale, is another famous wooden figure also from a bog, this time at Ballachulish in western Scotland. It looks to us quite grim, but is that how an Iron Age person would have seen it? At one level the answer is 'no' for, as found, the figure was covered with wickerwork, its face invisible; but perhaps such treatment was special to its deposition in water? Visible or not, was the face worshipped and, if so, how? And what were the expectations of the worshipper? We can but guess whether his beliefs and religious hopes were optimistic and buoyant, an assertion of life in a complex but manageable world, or a defensive, delaying act in a hostile world that would sooner or later overwhelm him.

Most photographable sites of prehistoric worship and belief are meaningless to us in terms of their original symbolism; their iconography is dead. We can speculate about stone circles, stone rows and single stones but we really have little idea of their significance in the minds of their builders. Were they purely symbolic, shutting out reality or enclosing sanctity? Was their symbolism of a different sort, representing woodland clearings and individual trees among communities of farmers who had cleared the land but whose roots still lay in the forests? Perhaps they symbolise, or actually represent, knowledge of the greatest of visible mysteries to people living much of their lives in the open, the skies. Certainly some alignments make sense in terms of the movement of the sun and possibly the moon, though we cannot subscribe to what appear to us the wilder flights of interpretative fancy concerning extensive relationships between such monuments and astronomy. Similarly, modern-day convictions about alleged former beliefs relating to the magical and mysterious properties of apparently non-utilitarian structures and their siting are unconvincing, but they are not necessarily wrong because they are unscientific. We often cannot know when we have stumbled on a fragment of proper understanding. Nevertheless, romantic nonsense is romantic nonsense, irrelevant to the people of prehistory, even if shafts of illumination may well come in the future from the serious study of the paranormal.

In terms of structures, the most obvious witnesses to belief over the millennia are burial mounds. For all we know, however, burial may have been secondary to their main purpose. They should perhaps be regarded more as field chapels or even churches; certainly the megalithic tombs which can be entered can be interpreted in this light. At some of them, evidence of elaborate ceremonial has been found at the entrances and inside. We can observe inhumation and cremation, we can infer excarnation, the exposure of corpses to the elements until all the flesh and sinews had decayed. We can even see the sophisticated details of construction in long and round barrows as, in themselves, part of an act of worship. But why the builders or worshippers acted as they did, we simply do not know. Faced with evidence such as the remains of sea-eagles at Isbister chambered cairn in Orkney, we can only hazard that some sort of contemporary statement of group identity is being made rather than just an offering to a deity.

In the fourth millennium BC the first great barrows were built, both megalithic and similar constructions in wood and earth. They may well have served several purposes simultaneously – marking a boundary, invoking the blessing of an external power on the land, creating a centre of ancestor-worship – but with very few exceptions they were also used for burial. Such inhumation in the same mausoleum or charnel house – if either is the correct analogy – was both in common and long-lived. Unless all the burials in one tomb were indeed from one family or other closed group, interment does not seem to have been private. You could expect to be joined in death for some time to come by the bones of the children of your neighbours and of their children's children.

Such preparation of the dead, and the deposition of their mortal remains in major buildings, might imply the worship of some non-human power or being, and it can be interpreted as evidence for some belief in an afterlife. Judging from the, to our eyes disrespectful, way in which skeletons were treated however, the idea may have been that afterlife was non-corporeal, maybe entirely spiritual or cerebral. In contrast, from about 2000 BC for at least 500 years, the earthly goods placed with the dead, cremated as well as inhumed, in essentially private burials beneath round barrows clearly imply faith in the idea of some further existence in which such would be needed. But, again, is this necessarily the right interpretation? Even today, the tradition at funerals of seeing the deceased off in appropriate manner is often not far from the surface of supposedly gloomy proceedings. Whereas we may choose to spend cash on public display rather than bury riches, in very different social and religious surroundings it may well have been that the manner of the going, judged by the community in status terms by the family or the group being able to *afford* the conspicuous waste of burying valuable metal equipment and jewellery, was more important than any deep thoughts about further use for such items. A similar approach to interpretation can be adopted with regard to the staggeringly rich cart-burials found beneath a few of the thousands of small barrows built on the Yorkshire Wolds in the last centuries BC. Arguably, archaeology seems to be pointing to explanation in the field of worldly status quite as much as other-worldly preparedness.

Speculation is clearly unavoidable in thinking about beliefs in the past. In the first millennium we can detect changes, even if what lay behind them is guesswork. Various 'cults' are attested: of the human head, of various animals especially the boar and the bull, and of water spirits on river bank, lakeside and at springs. Indeed, the realm of belief in the later centuries BC generally exudes a flavour of earthy naturalism, of vibrant animalism, of a conception of the world of Nature as a whole in which people were a part (but possibly distinguished by their ability to think?). It is, too, from this world that come echoes, just, in our contemporary, heavily Christianised calendar; of coincidences in time such as the festival of Samain, when spirits become visible to earthlings, with All Souls' or Martinmas in early November; or of Imbolc, a celebration of fertility, with Candlemas early in February.

Archaeologically, from the last centuries BC, we have both rectangular and circular buildings identified as shrines, in hillforts such as South Cadbury and Maiden Castle, and in the open, as at Frilford, Oxfordshire. Shafts, too, seem to have been part of the late prehistoric

Mayburgh henge monument near Penrith, Cumbria, here seen looking north-west obliquely through the single entrance on the east towards the central standing stone. The great surrounding bank of river pebbles, some 110 m in diameter crest to crest, curves from the foreground leftwards in an arc to complete the circuit on the west, north, and north-eastern sides. The area enclosed is 0.6 hectares, the bank up to 5 m high; the standing stone is the survivor of four, and four more stood in the entrance. The river is close by, to the right, providing a characteristic situation for this ceremonial-cum-religious centre of the later second millennium BC. Another such monument, called King Arthur's Round Table, lies 400 m east, the scene in the eighteenth century of rustic 'military exercises'.

ritual response, presumably giving access in some way to the underworld. And, in the first centuries BC and AD, there were Druids too, members of a powerful priesthood which seems to have presided over some naturalistic religion of the woods. Their practices involved human sacrifice, their observances wooden figures, their rites mistletoe. Even today we use mistletoe at our celebration of the two-thousand-year-old Christian Nativity, giggling at its sexual implications without realising we are but perpetuating, as the pagan year pivots around the time of the Midwinter Solstice, Druidic symbolism for animal fecundity.

On Knap Hill, Wiltshire, are the low but sharply defined earthworks of a banked and ditched enclosure of c 3000 BC, here viewed from near the route of the Ridgeway to its north-west. Gatherings probably took place on this hill some 5000 years ago, probably involving ritual and, therefore, enshrining the beliefs of the local population; but, equally, people perhaps lived and worked on this hilltop — and they may even have defended it. The bank is broken by five gaps, each fronted by a causeway of undug chalk across the line of the outer ditch, itself as much as 3 m deep in places. Adams Grave, a broadly contemporary megalithic tomb, lies on the skyline immediately west while two other Neolithic hilltop enclosures are not far away: Windmill Hill 8 km to the north, and Rybury 4 km to the west, partly beneath the earthworks of an Iron Age hillfort. People also lived on Knap Hill in Roman and medieval times.

Duggleby Howe in North Yorkshire, here shown in its landscape context looking south-south-west, was for long archaeologically well-known as an unusual and very large (c 6 m high and 37 m in diameter) Neolithic round barrow, apparently isolated on the Wolds. Air photography has now shown it to be in the centre of a completely ploughed-out henge monument. Possibly the now flattened bank and ditch of the henge were built around a specially important burial place; but the alternative sequence, of the barrow being built inside an enclosure already sanctified in some way, seems more likely. Either way, the mound was heaped up over a pit-burial of ten inhumations, after which it was used as the site for a cemetery with as many as a hundred cremations inserted into it.

The common type of burial structure belonging to the early farming communities in the fourth and third millennia BC is a long mound. Many were built in upland Britain, often using large stones for their internal structures and so in time attracting the attention of early antiquaries. Capel Garmon chambered tomb, Betws-y-Coed, Gwynedd, here seen looking north, gives a good idea of the type. It has a wedge-shaped mound some 28 m long, 13 m wide at its broader, eastern end (to the right) where stones outline a false entrance. The real entrance was halfway along the south side, giving into a 5 m long passage which led to a small central chamber with larger chambers to right and left. That on the left is still covered by its capstone. Most chambered tombs, however different they may look, basically display variations on the elements seen here.

Most people who go to see these great Neolithic monuments understandably visit the showpiece megalithic tombs maintained for public benefit by State agencies. Such sites are looked after immaculately in most cases, usually in a consolidated, sometimes in a restored, condition. They cannot, however, give much idea of the appearance of the far greater number of their counterparts which are not being cared for. This is one reason why even interested people do not recognise comparable sites and find it difficult to believe that, for every one of the 'show sites', there are or were, in the case of chambered long barrows, hundreds of similar monuments. This is Rubh'an Dunain chambered cairn, Skye, looking west at its exposed, damaged and unconsolidated façade and recessed entrance as left after excavations back in the early 1930s.

This view, in marked contrast with the last, shows the restored forecourt at the north-east end of a long cairn at Camster, Watten, Caithness. It is almost 70 m long. In the foreground, the southerly of two projections end on to the mound give the impression of 'horns' in plan. Supposedly these indicated, falsely, the entrance. As at Capel Garmon, the entrance is actually in the long side on the left, providing access into the mound at the level of a plinth and leading to a small, five-sided burial chamber. In fact the deception is greater still, for there are two entrances on the south side. The second one is out of sight here but it too led into a chamber, this time divided into three compartments. Recent excavation has shown that this complex and sophisticated structure began as two separate round cairns containing these chambers; both the round cairns were then enveloped within a single long structure with its new but deceptive, and now restored, eastern façade.

Another totally restored façade is that of the chambered long barrow at Wayland's Smithy on the Ridgeway near Uffington Castle, Oxfordshire, here viewed looking north-north-west. A well-known and much visited site, the façade, chambers and stone-revetted mound were shown by excavation to have succeeded, in the middle of the fourth millennium BC, earlier and different structural arrangements for the housing of the dead. Sadly or otherwise, the excavations produced no evidence to support the legend that Wayland, a metalworker and armourer with supernatural powers in Norse mythology, here later an invisible blacksmith, shoed horses for cash on the nail. The legend is nonetheless of some antiquity, the site being referred to as 'Welandes smidde' in a charter of AD 855.

(Opposite page) Trethevy Quoit, St Clear, Liskeard, Cornwall, viewed from the east is both impressive and a rare type of structure in the east of the county. Remains like this look more enigmatic than they actually are. This is no more than the burial chamber of a round cairn that was originally heaped over it but came to be removed in modern times. The remains of that mound were recorded as still the equivalent of 40 m by 18 m in the nineteenth century. The chamber itself is virtually a rectangular box of eight stones, 2 m by 1.5 m in plan and over 3 m high at its highest point. The tallest upright granite boulder (nearest the camera) seems both to divide the burial chamber and to mark the entrance into an inner chamber; its lower part is broken away to allow access. The capstone is 3.7 m long and holed at its highest corner. Curiously, no finds are recorded and no folklore has attached itself to the site.

Stoney Littleton long barrow, Avon, a few miles south of Bath, has an entrance at the narrow end of its incurved forecourt. The drystone walling of Jurassic limestone sets off the Blue Lias stones which form the lintel and two jambs, one bearing an ammonite 0.31 m in diameter (ARIETITES sp.). Beyond, off a passage, lie three pairs of side chambers and an end chamber. Whatever the fossil imprint may have signified to those who used the monument in the third millennium BC, the site meant a lot to the local rector, John Skinner, in the early nineteenth century AD. His digging of it brought him into contact with the antiquarian Sir Richard Colt Hoare of Stourhead, much to Skinner's gratification. He later committed suicide, despairing of his drunken flock and plagued by persecution mania. About one hundred manuscript volumes of his diaries and notes are in the British Museum.

Excavation has often shown that burial places, once chosen, remain in use over long periods. The five-phase structure on Cairnpapple Hill, Torpichen, West Lothian, was an irregular arc of seven burial pits near a setting of three large stones in the early centuries of the third millennium BC. It then became a henge monument containing a setting of twenty-four standing stones. Later its appearance and function were changed, the site being converted into successive burial mounds. The grave in this photograph, with its kerb, Beaker pot, and standing stone, was later subsumed into a large cairn built on top of the henge monument c 1900 BC. The latest mound in turn had graves inserted into it, probably in the early centuries AD.

Maen-y-Bardd dolmen, Roewen, Gwynedd, here seen looking north-north-east, is another burial chamber that was formerly inside a mound. The chamber is on top of a ruinous wall running down the slope from left to right. The wall therefore appears to be earlier than the dolmen and, since it is also part of a field system, this north Welsh hillside clearly proclaims itself a very early example of an organised landscape of the third millennium BC. Whatever the date, this chambered cairn joins others, for example in Ireland, Scilly and Orkney, in demonstrating that the places of the dead were not just isolated mounds but were part of an agriculturally developed countryside. Burial cairns may well have been built at particular points in such countryside for reasons of belief associating seasonal rebirth in the fields with existence after death.

(Opposite page) Another structurally complex cairn is Minning Low in Derbyshire, one of two cairns in the plantation seen here and the largest of the chambered tombs in the Peak District. The mound is 43 m by 37 m and 2.5 m high. Here we look south-west at the southern and eastern capstones of two chambers within the mound; it contains at least two others. No burials are recorded even though the site was subject to the attentions of one of the most vigorous of Victorian barrow-diggers, Thomas Bateman. It was, however, robbed during the Roman period, about 2000 years ago and some 3000 years after it was built.

(Previous page) Arbor Low, Middleton, also in the Derbyshire Peak District, is a henge monument with no later structural phases apart from a round barrow near its eastern entrance. From its southern entrance, as this photograph looking south-west shows, a low bank curves towards, but not actually to, Gib Hill barrow. This apparently consists of two mounds, a round one on top of an oval one, being a burial place of the third and second millennia BC, silhouetted on the skyline some 110 m away from the henge. The low bank is undated, though it is probably later, perhaps much later, than the henge monument. It might possibly be a link, physically surviving but of lost significance, between two adjacent sites of different functions each in its own way a monument to belief.

(Opposite) The visually prominent positions sought out as places for ceremony and burial are exemplified by this view looking south towards Pwllheli from Yr Eifl on the Lleyn Peninsula in north-west Wales. The Mynydd Carnguwch cairn, after which both the hill and the parish are named, is on the hilltop in the centre at 359 m above sea level. It is visible over a wide area to the south, the relatively low-lying farmlands from which it was designed to be seen. The cairn itself is oval, spread to a maximum 40 m in diameter; its core is surrounded by a near-vertical revetment of unshaped stones selected so that the larger blocks are at the bottom. The centre has been disturbed. Possibly all the stones outside the revetment were originally piled up within it to form a solid drum-shaped structure which would have been an even more striking feature in the landscape. The cairn has been identified by some as a medieval castle mound or an Iron Age mausoleum rather than a Bronze Age burial mound — but, either way, the point about the superb position remains.

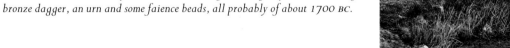

The burial mounds of the second millennium often form cemeteries, apparently placed in deliberate patterns. The Ashen Hill barrows, near Priddy, Somerset, here viewed from another barrow group, the Priddy Nine barrows, look as if they were built as a straight line along the crest of the hill. That is a deliberately contrived illusion, a Bronze Age coup d'oeil long before it was used as a device by landscape architects in the eighteenth century AD. We know why the latter adopted it; if only we knew what was in the minds of their counterparts in the eighteenth century BC. Were they just being clever or was the trick in some way an expression of their beliefs?

At other places, the obviously prominent local site was not used for a burial mound and we might almost come to suspect that artifice was attempting to mirror nature. We look north, to the left here, at Cheesering Tor on Bodmin Moor, Cornwall; on the right is one of the most famous burial mounds in British prehistory, the Rillaton barrow. It is 36 m in diameter and almost 2.5 m high. The similarity of silhouette is partly false, for the barrow's derives in some measure from its disturbance in modern times. It has a large robbers' pit in its top and a prehistoric grave, rebuilt about 1890 AD, on its east. It was the contents of that grave, excavated in 1837, which brought the barrow fame, for in it lay the famous 'Rillaton gold cup', a handled beaker of corrugated sheet gold now in the British Museum. It accompanied a skeleton in a funereal group also containing a bronze dagger, an urn and some faience beads, all probably of about 1700 BC.

Modern excavation has often shown round cairns to be long-lived and structurally complex. One notable example is at Brenig, Mynydd Hiraethog, in Clwyd, North Wales, where excavations were carried out in the 1970s before the flooding of the Fechan valley for a reservoir. Some of the sites examined have been restored, like that in the photograph, and an archaeological trail for visitors created. This is a type of structure called a platform cairn, here built on top of an earlier habitation site also of the second millennium BC. Was that coincidence deliberate or accidental? Essentially, this stone monument consists of a low, circular platform enclosing an open central area; beneath the platform were the cremated ashes of an adult and a child in an urn below a stone, while in the central enclosure stood a large post. The enclosure was eventually filled in with stones and, later, a small mound was added to cover an urn on the part of the platform nearest the camera. It was precisely this sort of structural complexity that was missed by the primitive archaeological techniques of the early barrow diggers.

(Opposite page) People were not generally buried under mounds in the first millennium BC but an exception is the small, low and sometimes square type of barrow which probably represents an immigrant population coming direct to the Yorkshire Wolds from north-west France in the middle of the second century BC. Most of the earthwork evidence of these late Iron Age barrow-cemeteries has now been destroyed, much of it during the intensification of agriculture in the last thirty years, but some barrows can still be seen at what may well have been the largest of these cemeteries, Danes Graves, Driffield, in Humberside. That this photograph was taken in a wood is no accident: the situation has preserved the mounds, left foreground and centre right. Originally about 500 existed. Their name is, of course, no more than an attribution made in ignorance before the advent of scientific archaeology in an area where anything difficult of explanation was put down to the Vikings.

The Rudston monolith on the Wolds, now in North Humberside, is the tallest prehistoric standing stone in Britain. Some 7.7 m high even though the top is now broken, its historical interest is that a church was built beside it and a churchyard around it, suggesting the possibility of continuity of worship if not of belief on the site. Archaeologically its context is a dense concentration of prehistoric monuments around Rudston village; it may well have been deliberately related to any one, or all, of three nearby cursuses — elongated, parallel-sided Neolithic enclosures. The monolith itself was enclosed within a ditched rectangle; originally another, smaller monolith stood to its east. It is of gritstone, weighs c 26 tonnes, and was transported to this spot from Cayton Bay, 16 km to the north near Scarborough, probably within a century or two of 2000 BC.

The Devil's Arrows at Boroughbridge, North Yorkshire, are also of gritstone and were also dragged here overland, though only about 10 km in this case, probably from Knaresborough. Visible to motorists from the A1, the three monoliths form a near straight line directed towards a ford across the River Ure. The stone in the foreground is c 6 m high, the two further ones to the south-east c 7 m each. The fluting is natural, the result of weathering. Again, these monoliths were not isolated in their original context for there were other monuments, now destroyed, in the area around 2000 BC. There was a fourth stone in this row. The attribution of the inexplicable to the Devil is, of course, not uncommon; in this case, he was supposedly shooting at Aldborough but fell short, though not by much considering he was supposedly standing on How Hill some 13 km to the west.

(Above) An alignment of three monoliths again in a lowland setting, Harold's Stones at Trellech, near Monmouth in Gwent, convey what many would take as mysterious dereliction, at least when seen on an autumnal day of mist and rain. The central stone in this row, which is only 12 m long, may have been shaped; it bears two cup marks on its south side. Here we are looking north towards the church of Trellech village, a name which itself means 'the village of stones'. In this case, at least three stories attach to the Stones: they are immovable; they dropped here in a megalithic stone-throwing competition between the Devil and the magician Jack o' Kent; they commemorate victory in a battle fought by Harold at Trellech. Their prehistoric date is assumed but not proven by excavation.

At Merrivale on Dartmoor stand, in contrast, two long rows of short stones, not quite parallel but seemingly ranged side by side on purpose. Deliberation too must have determined the small size of stone used in these rows: large boulders abound in the area so the megalithic understatement made by these rows is clearly by choice. Other broadly contemporary structures, including a stone circle, exist in the immediate vicinity. Here we look east. The northern row is 180 m long, that on the right 259 m; each row is double, consisting of two parallel lines of upright stones. A larger stone stands at the eastern end of both rows, while a small circle of stones lies about halfway along the southern alignment. The rows are undated but probably belong to the centuries immediately after 2000 BC. What they were for is unknown and any suggestions are but guesses.

Some sites do seem to represent regional ceremonial centres. An outstanding example is on Moss Farm along the south side of Machrie Water on the Isle of Arran, one of the most remarkable concentrations in Britain of stone monuments surviving from the centuries around 2000 BC. Survival is in part due to the peat which has subsequently enveloped the site: one 'new' stone circle has recently emerged from the shrinking bog to join the five already known along less than 0.5 km of farm track. Here we gain an impression of the closeness, looking east from one of the circles containing a dramatic, but naturally weathered, upright stone towards another circle with three of the tallest monoliths (up to 5.5 m high) in a British stone circle other than Stonehenge and Avebury.

(Above) The eighteenth-century antiquary William Stukeley recognised another type of ceremonial monument which he called a cursus. Known mainly in southern and eastern England, these embanked and ditched enclosures, often several hundred metres long and of third millennium date, together represent a tremendous building achievement. One of the best surviving lengths, paralleled by a flattened counterpart 90 m to its north, is this bank with a ditch on its left, part of the exceptionally long (9.6 km) Dorset cursus, here crossing Bottlebush Down on Cranborne Chase. Its function is unknown but an association with death, ceremony and landscape organisation seems legitimate speculation.

The main stone circle at Callanish on Lewis among Scotland's Western Isles is one of the most striking of all British antiquities. Preservation of the structures is again due to peat which covered some, and partly covered others, until the last century. The stone circle here, one of several in the area, overlooks Loch Roag, its thirteen stones arranged in a circle only 5 m in diameter. The central upright is 4.75 m high and is set into the western side of a small chambered cairn. The uprights of its passage and chamber can be seen on the monolith's left. Outside, the circle is approached by (or has radiating from it) an avenue of stones on the north, with single lines of stones to east, south and west. Unfortunately, factual description can convey little of the site's ambience nor can it go very far in explaining it. Meaningless though the arrangements are to us, they presumably embody a complex symbolism and pattern of beliefs.

(Previous page) Such is our ignorance of their meaning that many stone circles do not look very impressive; we can only assume that their significance lay in their symbolism c 2000 BC rather than appearance alone. There appears to be little attempt at visual drama in the Torhouskie stone circle near Wigtown, Dumfries and Galloway, yet it exhibits a certain precision. The site is on a low platform; as at other circles, the nineteen granite boulders appear to have been selected for height and then placed, in a graded sequence towards the highest stones, in a flattened arc of the circle on the south-east; and they are faced by a line of three boulders near the centre. A standing stone faces the circle 24 m to the south, and nearby to the east is a short row of three stones. We can note this apparent interest in vertical and horizontal patterning but only guess at its significance.

The Yellowmead 'stone circle', near Sheepstor on the south-western edge of Dartmoor, looks enigmatic but only if judged as a quadruple circle of standing stones. The circles are actually the kerb-stones within and around the circumference of a burial cairn of which only traces now remain. The diameter of the outer circle is 20 m; its stones appear to have been carefully chosen to be larger than those in the other circles, the diameters of which are, respectively, 15, 12 and 6 m. The twenty-one stones of the innermost kerb are almost touching each other. The monument as we see it was created in 1921 when the stones were re-erected following the discovery of the site earlier that year in drought conditions after heather-burning. Traces of a double stone row extend to the west, crossed by what appears to be a bank and ditch. This is a disused leat, medieval or later, which probably carried water to tinworks in the area.

(Opposite page) Nine Stones Close stone circle, on Harthill Moor, Derbyshire, now consists of four uprights, the largest boulders used in any of the county's prehistoric monuments and the remains of a circle originally c 13 m in diameter. Like most other excavations at stone circles, this produced little in the way of finds – a few potsherds and a worked flint – when dug by Thomas Bateman in 1847. Robin Hood's Stride is the hillock in the background and, although the site appears to be isolated near the eastern edge of the Limestone above the River Derwent, a little further west and south on higher ground is plentiful evidence of contemporary and later prehistoric activity.

The Fourstones near Duddo in Northumberland are the remains of a stone circle originally some 10 m in diameter. Even now, five stones still stand; they are all of the local sandstone and c 2 m in height. The site occupies a minor watershed position between the Rivers Till and Tweed on the top of a low knoll in low-lying ground, now accentuated by cultivation of the surrounding fields which has come right up to its edge. This area of north Northumberland has few major monuments in stone from the later third/earlier second millennia, but lies not far from a concentration of broadly contemporary earth and timber constructions in the Milfield Basin north of Wooler.

The Rollright Stones stand on the Cotswolds close to the Oxfordshire/Warwickshire county boundary. The circle itself, the King's Men, is 31.6 m in diameter and consists of an apparently variable number of heavily weathered blocks of oolitic limestone projecting an aura of considerable antiquity. Some 73 m to the north-east is the King Stone, a monolith; 360 m east-south-east are the Whispering Knights, the remains of a chambered long barrow. Folklore, ignoring the different dates of these structures, relates a dozen different stories. One decrees that it is impossible to count the stones in the circle: of four modern accounts, two give 53–4 and 77 respectively, a third shows 28 possibly in position, while the fourth cites 66 and judges that there were about 22 originally.

(Right) The Stanton Drew stone circles in Avon are not well known but are almost of Avebury proportions. Here we look north-west at three of the stones of the north-east circle, solid blocks of the local dolomitic conglomerate. The complex contains three circles, the central 'Great Circle' consisting almost entirely of fallen stones; two avenues of stone, both running east; a 'Cove' as at Avebury; and an outlying stone, Hauteville's Quoit, located to the north-east as at Rollright. This great and almost certainly long-lived ceremonial centre was probably contemporary with Avebury in the second half of the third millennium BC. Here again folklore decrees that the stones are uncountable.

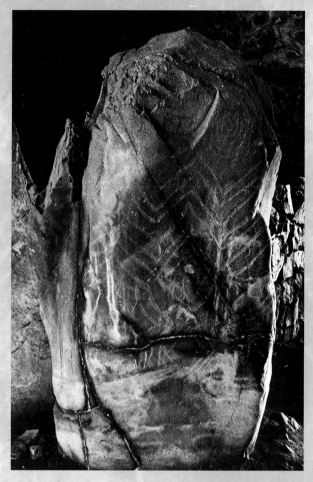

This decorated upright stone in the accessible burial chamber of Barclodiad-y-Gawres in Anglesey is quite exceptional for 'mainland' Britain, though it would not be remarkable on the other side of the Irish Sea or in Brittany. It must have symbolised something to its beholders around 3000 BC; our impression, after flashlight and torchlight examination in the funereal gloom, was that through the use of non-representational art it had been humanised.

One of the more remarkable manifestations of the human mind in prehistoric Britain is the rock-art liberally scattered across slabs of exposed stone particularly in northern England and southern Scotland. This natural outcrop of sandstone at Roughting Linn near Lowick, Northumberland, bears one of the larger works of prehistoric British art, dating to about 2000 BC. In all there are several dozen figures though they do not form, to our eyes, a composition. The prominent circle with vertical line left centre is 559 mm across while that to its right is older than the cleavage in the rock which cuts it. The site lies near a waterfall and just outside much later defences.

(Right) A common practice, particularly in Northumberland as here on Dod Law near Wooler, was to enclose cup-marks in subrectangular shapes defined by one or more grooves. Ever attracted by simple explanations, some have suggested that such designs might be representational, for they are comparable to the plans of late prehistoric enclosed settlements in the area. Other difficulties apart, however, the petroglyphs are likely to be at least a thousand years earlier than the settlements in question.

(Opposite page) Rock-art is not always exposed now though it undoubtedly was in the third and second millennia. Sometimes, for example, peat has covered and protected the work, so more is always liable to be uncovered. One area where this has happened recently is on Ilkley Moor, West Yorkshire, adding to the fairly large body of material already known. Here is just one example: the Hanging Stones, showing a characteristic pattern of pecked lines, meaningless to us but presumably full of significance in 1981 BC (compare the work of our own day, bottom right).

(Left) Pecked patterns are even more extensive at Achnabreck in Mid Argyll. This is part of one of two large surfaces of natural rock liberally covered with what at first glance is a bewildering complex of 'art'; in fact the repertoire is basically restricted to cup-marks, that is, circular indentations, and grooved circles and lines with some spirals. The circular 'spider's web' motif in the centre of the photograph is 1 m in diameter and typically consists of a central cup-mark within roughly concentric grooves, here with radiating lines too. The striations are glacial scratches.

Variants on the enclosed cup-marks motif are here seen at Ormaig near Kilmartin, Argyll, not far from Achnabreck. This is another of the major rock sheets of prehistoric Britain. Most of the symbols are simple cup-marks but some of them are surrounded by grooves. The unusual motif is the cup-mark surrounded by a ring of smaller cup-marks enclosed by an outer groove. We can, indeed, guess that all these designs were executed within a known frame of symbolism and reference and that they did convey messages of some sort to those who saw them; but whether such meanings were practical, indicating routes or boundaries for example, or ideological we can only speculate. Though they appear to us to be non-representational, it is unlikely that they are a form of abstract art in the sense that the term is used today.

Several white horses face the world from the scarps of the Wessex Downs, but all are of the eighteenth, nineteenth and early twentieth centuries. The Westbury White Horse, Wiltshire, is stylistically typical in its rather inanimate podginess. It was produced by a Mr Gee in the later eighteenth century. But he was remodelling an existing chalk-cut horse so it is just possible that this early Westbury figure was originally prehistoric too, a thought tantalisingly hinted at by the un-Georgian neck and head seen here. Nor can we totally dismiss the argument for its origin in the ninth/tenth centuries AD, as is also claimed for Uffington. Both places are in areas important to King Alfred.

(Left) The outstanding example of an artistic landscape statement is the Uffington White Horse on the northern scarp of the Wessex Downs in Oxfordshire, a miracle of survival whether or not it is prehistoric in origin. Similar to horses on coins and metalwork of the century before the Roman conquest, it is so idiosyncratic that a later date is unlikely unless it was copied. It existed in late Anglo-Saxon times. Here we look north across its head towards the Upper Thames Valley and, at the bottom of the scarp, Dragon Hill, a natural knoll with an artificially flattened top where traditionally St George slew the dragon.

The date of this human head is uncertain too but it could well represent the paganism of the last centuries in pre-Roman Britain and of later times in areas beyond Roman cultural domination. That paganism expressed itself in many ways, not all of which have left material traces; druids in oak groves could be one of them. Certainly animals were involved, and so too was the human head: we have real and surrogate evidence of that. This head is cemented into a wall at Hendy Farm near the Menai Bridge, Anglesey. To interpret it for our world, we can characterise as 'Celtic' its angular nose, small, slit mouth and hollowed cranium; but in its enigmatic half-smile, this face from another world is blandly secretive.

PREHISTORY IN LANDSCAPES

Prehistoric man had, and still has, a considerable effect on the landscape. We can see this today, often perhaps without realising, in the appearance of a stretch of countryside, in its vegetation, in its pattern of farms, fields and lanes and, most obviously, in its monuments surviving from two thousand and more years ago.

Here we look at the same sorts of field evidence illustrated in *A portfolio from prehistory*, but from a different point of view. We have chosen four widely separated and contrasting areas – the Orkneys, Maen-y-Bardd in North Wales, the Avebury area in Wiltshire, and West Penwith in Cornwall – and illustrate a range of prehistoric sites from each. Our emphasis is on the character of each area, its local prehistory as it were, and we present the monuments primarily in the context of their locality. It then becomes possible to compare in different parts of Britain, firstly, variety in particular types of monument – burial cairns for example – and secondly, the extent to which the character of the surviving prehistory reflects the different nature of each of four contrasting areas.

A crucial caveat to enter about this approach is that we and, more importantly, others have studied these four areas in considerable detail. Here we can only cream off in visual terms the best and the most representative. Many, many more sites are known, and much, much more information is available than we are able to display and use here. Furthermore, prehistoric research is dynamic: in all four areas more waits to be discovered on and in the ground and, quite as importantly, new research and analysis continually refines our understanding. Even though we present the photographs in a local context, with some fine detail in places, our treatment is neither comprehensive nor is its subject static.

We carried out fieldwork in all four of our areas during 1987, collecting information and selecting not just individual sites for illustration but also specific views of them for later photography. Most of the photographs were therefore obtained during 1987–8, within a framework already conceived and specific to the needs of this chapter. Unlike *A portfolio from prehistory*, where an archaeological approach has, by and large, been superimposed on a carefully chosen selection of photographs from an existing collection, selection for *Prehistory in landscapes* was made in the field on archaeological criteria. The photography followed. The section is still highly selective but we have throughout tried to illustrate the typical and the mundane as well as the great and the good.

Between seventy and ninety islands make up the Orkney archipelago, about twenty of them little more than rocks. In prehistoric times there would, however, have been fewer islands for erosion and a slowly rising sea-level have fragmented some into separate entities. About twenty islands are now inhabited, the centre of Orcadian life being the largest island, somewhat confusingly for the outsider called Mainland. Its main town, Kirkwall, lies on its north coast just over 40 kms from the nearest point on the Caithness coast of Scotland.

A degree of cultural isolation imposed by the sea has been a signal factor in Orkney's history. Yet the maritime position of the islands has enabled them to receive cultural influences in a combination denied to other parts of Britain. Clearly their physical relationship to Scandinavia to the east, transformed into a cultural and political relationship in medieval times, has been significant; but Orkney is also strategically situated in relation to more domestic influences flowing south to north along the east and west coasts of Britain.

Archaeologically, a major feature of Orkney is its geology. Most of the land mass is Old Red Sandstone, rock with the particular characteristic that it splits off along more or less horizontal planes. Here was an ideal building material for prehistoric peoples which they exploited to the full; not just functionally, though thin, flat-sided rectangular slabs were ideal for building, but by *c* 3000 BC with increasing craftsmanship to create, quite deliberately, an aesthetic effect. The availability of a superb raw material, constructional ability, and aesthetic aspirations were the three factors which enabled prehistoric Orcadians to create their quite outstanding monumental achievement.

That there is so much to see today owes a lot to other factors too. Sites have survived well because of a relatively small population and generally unexpansive land use over the last two millennia. Indeed, much of the threat over the last two centuries has been antiquarian rather than agricultural. In the twentieth century, balancing that, a major factor for preservation has been, and is, the dedication of that distant arm of central government, the Inspectorate of Ancient Monuments.

The monuments of prehistoric Orkney first appear in the fourth millennium BC. Arguably, prehistory here continued into the thirteenth, even the fifteenth, century for it was 1468 AD before the Scottish Crown asserted its authority over the islands. Only the chronological limits of the book constrain us to end our survey in the early centuries AD.

Of all the remarkable burial structures of prehistoric Britain, the Dwarfie Stane on Hoy is in a class, literally, of its own. Here we see it from outside looking north-east. The Stane is a natural block of sandstone lying on open moorland at the foot of the precipitous Dwarfie Hamars to the south. Out of it has been hollowed, using only stone tools, a small chamber, apparently a tomb cut from the solid rock. A hole carved out of the side of the stone served as the entrance, originally closed by a blocking stone. This was still in position in the sixteenth century but now lies outside where it was left, presumably by those who first broke into the Stane.

Two small holes in the side of the Dwarfie Stane's hollowed interior gave into two side chambers over protruding sills. This interior view, looking south-east, shows these side chambers, with the uncut rock sill clearly visible on the right. The roof of the chamber beyond still bears the marks of the stone tools of the carvers. What was inside these chambers is unknown but the whole is assumed to have been a tomb, from its architectural features and because the entrance was closed by a stone. Construction probably belongs to the third millennium BC.

140

Maes Howe chambered cairn, Orkney Mainland, is considered by many archaeologists to be one of the great architectural achievements of prehistoric Europe, comparable to – but earlier than – Stonehenge III and the great megalithic tombs (tholoi) of Bronze Age Greece at Mycenae and Boiotia. It is a circular, cone-shaped mound, 35 m in diameter and 7 m high, surrounded by a ditch and a, mainly later, external bank. Built soon after 3000 BC, four thousand years later the interior was desecrated or enhanced, depending on your point of view, by Viking graffiti in the shape of runic writing and Norse art of the ninth–twelfth centuries AD. The paved entrance passage, on the south-west of the mound, is 11 m long, 1.4 m high and just less than a metre wide. Here we look along it towards the central chamber, 4.6 m square, the walls rising for 1.4 m, then stepping inwards course by course to a surviving original height of 3.8 m. Above is modern work.

Behind each wall of the central chamber at Maes Howe, except where the entrance passage emerges, is a side chamber; and at each corner is a projecting pier, the one here being on the north-west. Like the other three, it incorporates a large vertical monolith and demonstrates superb craftsmanship in the very fine masonry, here seen continuing up into the corbelling. In the foreground is the entrance into one of the three side chambers, almost 1 m above floor level, with the stone originally blocking it lying on the floor in front. The same feature occurs outside the other side chambers, all of which are rectangular, between c 1.4 and 2 m internally, about 1 metre high and roofed with a single slab.

(Above) The main chamber of the circular cairn on Cuween Hill, Orkney Mainland, 4.7 km due east of Maes Howe, displays masonry of comparable quality, here seen looking north-east. Entry is only possible on hands and knees along a passage into it. When it was originally examined in the nineteenth century, twenty-four dog skulls were lying on the chamber's floor. Four side chambers, one of two cells, are entered through separate portals, one in each wall; here the side of one entrance is in the left foreground and the two others visible are characteristically above floor level. The back wall of the rear cell can be seen through the central entrance. The whole structure seems less stable than Maes Howe for the tilt to the right is both real and ancient.

(Opposite page) Recognisably in the same architectural style but in chunkier construction is the central burial chamber of the prominent cairn on Vinquoy Hill, Eday. It was built of the local red sandstone in the third millennium BC. The entrance passage is partly subterranean and only c 3 m long. Again four side chambers lead off the main corbelled chamber; here the entrances to two of them can be seen, this time at floor level. The whole is less sophisticated than Maes Howe and Cuween on Orkney Mainland and, though impressive in terms of the effort involved in placing the building stones, the craftsmanship is cruder. The site has recently been re-excavated and partly reconstructed as part of the Eday Heritage Walk established in 1986 in a co-operative venture 'to enable visitors to explore the many places of interest at the north end of Eday'. The view from Vinquoy is superb.

Quoyness chambered cairn, Sanday, is another Maes Howe type of tomb, though from outside looking west-north-west it looks rather like a fortification. This is the result of its elaborate construction and the chaotic way in which it was excavated last century; both have determined the manner in which it is presented now. Basically it consists of a revetted, artificial platform, as at Maes Howe, here crossed by the path in the foreground. On this were built three roughly concentric drystone wall-faces, the outermost around the base of the mound, the middle one in the mound, the innermost encasing the burial chambers. The last two are the ones visible here, together with the revetment flanking the entrance passage leading down into a central chamber with six side chambers.

Originally the passage at Quoyness was 9 m long and only 0.6 m high, making it necessary, as at Cuween, to crawl into the tomb. The architectural effect and the style of masonry echo other Orkney chambered tombs: here we see the narrowing of the chamber towards its full original height of 4 m, with three entrances to side chambers at floor level. The pit in the left-hand corner contained a burial in a cist and four of the side chambers contained burials. Other finds of stone and bone implements similar to material from Skara Brae suggest its original date was early in the third millennium. The area around continued, however, to be used as a cemetery into the second millennium BC.

Midhowe chambered cairn, Rousay, is broadly of the same period in the third millennium as Maes Howe but is structurally very different. It consists of a long mound bisected by a central, elongated burial chamber subdivided by upright flagstones into opposed stalls separated longitudinally by a walkway. Here we are looking south-east along the full length of the internal chamber, from the terminal burial cell in the foreground to the short entrance, or exit, passage at the far end. The side walls survive to a height of 2.5 m but the whole of the roof has been removed. Corpses for burial were placed on or under low benches in the compartments. The length of the cairn visible here is c 25 m; the whole mound is 32.5 m long and c 13 m wide. It is situated on low-lying ground by the sea and was part of a Neolithic agricultural landscape for field walls branch off from its two eastern corners. The whole monument is now encased in a steel-framed hangar for display.

Holm of Papa Westray, a small island off the eastern side of Papa Westray, was probably a promontory of the main island when the chambered cairn which today dominates its southern end was built in the early third millennium BC. The mound is some 35 m long with a protruding 'conning tower' on top serving as the modern entrance. Inside, here shown looking north-east, is a narrow chamber 20.5 m long with ten side chambers and a terminal chamber at each end. The photograph shows three of the entrances to the side chambers, with one of the end chambers beneath the low lintel beyond. The masonry is particularly fine. The Holm, still only accessible by small boat, contains another cairn, recently excavated, fragments of ancient field walls, a geometrical pattern of (possibly anti-glider) ditches, and a thrivingly raucous sea-bird population.

(Above) A detail inside the Holm of Papa Westray chambered cairn shows a rare example of a decorated lintel above the entrance to the most south-easterly of the side chambers. Here the pecked dots and arcs are combined in an 'eye-brow' motif known elsewhere in megalithic art, notably in Irish chambered tombs. Other examples exist in the tomb, both in this chamber on the opposite wall, as circles and zig-zags, and in the central chamber just south of the entrance.

(Left) Unstan chambered round cairn lies low on the southern shore of the Loch of Stenness. Its entrance passage on the east, c 6 m long through three rings of retaining wall, leads to an approximately rectangular central chamber, set at right angles with a cell at each end. The chamber is divided into three pairs of opposed stalls. This view is of two of those stalls and, between the portals of the southern end chamber, of the large stone which characteristically terminates the whole central chamber. The stalls contained skeletal remains and fragments of at least thirty-five different pottery bowls also occurred. The cairn, now protected by a modern concrete roof, looks like an upturned pudding bowl.

The chambered cairn on Wideford Hill, Mainland, is set into a fairly steep north-west-facing slope at 125 m above sea level. It looks out over the relatively fertile coastland around the Bay of Firth. Below it are the Quanterness tomb, of Maes Howe type and c 3400 BC date, and over to the west the Cuween tomb. The Wideford Hill tomb was built in a tripartite, concentric ring structure with a low, narrow entrance passage coming slightly uphill into a central chamber with three side chambers. The original entrance is unsuitable for the bulk of twentieth-century man so modern access is, somewhat confusingly, by a trapdoor and ladder down to the top of the central chamber.

The alliteratively named chambered cairn of Taversoe Tuick, Trumland, is the most easterly of the cairns strung along the narrow, south-facing coastal strip between Midhowe and the ferry pier at Brinyan on Rousay. Its main interest is its 'double-decker' structure: to all intents and purposes one cairn is built on top of another. The earlier has a 12 m long passage from the south-east leading into a kidney-shaped chamber divided into four small compartments. The photograph shows its western end with one benched compartment on the right for a corpse. Immediately above the roof here is the segmented chamber of the second cairn.

These are the doorways used by people who, during their lifetimes, perhaps helped build a chambered cairn and possibly even hoped to be buried in one. The site is called Knap of Howar; it is on Papa Westray, one of the most fertile of the Orkney islands. Here we see the front of two buildings, their original, dry-stone walls still standing up to 1.62 m high. On the right is the house, on the left the structurally later but connected workshed-cum-storehouse. The doorways face north-west on to the shore now but, five thousand years ago, probably gave on to open grassland behind a dune system. These domestic buildings were built and were in use between c 3500–2800 BC. To be able to study both domestic and funeral structures of this period in the same area is a privilege unique in north-western Europe.

(Below) This view of the more northerly of the Knap of Howar build-ings is from the top of the wall just left of the left hand doorway in the preceding photograph. This is the interior of a Neolithic home with at least some of its fittings and furnishings. The building is divided into three. In the foreground is a lobby area, just inside the outer door and giving on to the short passage connecting with the slightly earlier house next door. Beyond the remains of the first inner stone partition is a hearth, mortar stone and group of wall-recesses; while beyond again, past the second partition, is a smaller room with wall cupboards (out of sight behind the right-hand upright). The whole structure was cut into a rubbish heap so, early though it is, people were certainly living on the site before this house was built.

Skara Brae, much better known than Knap of Howar, is the other well-preserved Neolithic settlement on Orkney. It is justifiably the mecca for many tourists. Because most of the remains are beneath their feet, they can easily gain the impression of houses and other structures cut down into a huge midden, eventually buried by the formation of sand-dunes and so preserved. The settlement we see today probably did not originate quite as early as the Knap of Howar for here occupation spanned the first half of the third millennium BC. Most views of House 7 are from above, looking down from present ground level. Here the view is from its doorway at prehistoric ground level, looking the length of the main room across the clean sand floor and central hearth towards one of the famous Skara Brae stone dressers against the far wall. This exhibits, not by accident and therefore presumably for aesthetic reasons, two vertical straight joints symmetrical to the dresser.

As Skara Brae developed into quite a large and elaborate settlement, it became necessary to make organised routes between the numerous buildings. They were interconnected below ground by what were in effect narrow tunnels. Below we look north-east along the main one from its junction with a side path by the entrance into one of the houses. The entrance into another house is just beyond the kink in the main passage. Though cruder than the best masonry in the entrance passages to the chambered cairns, the style and architectural effect here is not dissimilar from that of contemporary tombs. We can imagine bustle and noise as well as the pervasive smells of woodsmoke and probably not very clean humanity.

Another straight joint, top left, indicates the sort of continual modification that must have been common in the buildings of a settlement such as Skara Brae as the needs and numbers of the inhabitants changed, and as the stresses and strains on the buildings themselves varied over the centuries. This detail in House 7 shows a characteristic wall-recess, apparently halved in width at some stage (did the original lintel snap?). It was made, presumably as a very deliberate act to improve comfort, immediately above another common fitting, a box-bed, which the 'cupboard in the wall' perhaps served in the manner of the bedside table in a modern house. Filled with straw or heather and covered with a cow-hide (Neolithic Orcadians did not know how to weave), the bed itself would have been more comfortable than it suggests in its bare and unmade-up state. Nowhere else in Britain does domestic detail of this quality survive from the centuries around 2700 BC.

(Opposite page) The Ring of Brodgar, here seen looking north-west into the setting sun on a fine summer's evening, is a circular stone setting c 104 m in diameter, round the inner side of a ditch with two entrances. Of about sixty original monoliths, twenty-seven exist but thirteen have been re-erected since the mid-nineteenth century; they are between 2–4.5 m high. The ditch, c 10 m wide and 3 m deep, involved the removal elsewhere of c 4,700 cubic metres of rock. Centre left is a later round barrow. In the twelfth century, Bjorn, a Norse visitor, carved his name in runes on one of the standing stones.

The Stones of Stenness on the shores of the Lochs of Stenness and Harray are central to an elaborate concentration of monuments dating to about 3000–2500 BC. The Watch Stone, 5.6 m high and visible in the photograph just to the left of the right-hand stone, is only 170 m to the north-north-west. The three stones are part of a former circle, probably of twelve uprights and c 30 m in diameter, at the centre of which was a setting of horizontal stones. The stone circle was enclosed by a ditch, 7 m wide and 2 m deep, and outer bank c 44 m in diameter with a single entrance on the north. This henge monument has been largely flattened by cultivation but traces of it can be seen on the left.

(Left) Far from the deliberate grandeur of the Stones of Stenness but nevertheless important in their unpretentious way, these stones are the remains of a prehistoric field wall. Probably in the second millennium BC, they served as a land-division, bounding individual fields or marking out larger units as part of an apparently extensive pattern of ancient boundaries over the north-west of the island of Eday. Gradually this ancient enclosed landscape was engulfed by peat, stopping the farming but preserving its structures and creating today's treeless, heather-dominated scenery on the western slopes of Noup Hill at the north end of the island. The wall was accidentally uncovered during peat-cutting by hand.

Beautifully located looking over Eynhallow Sound towards Rousay, Gurness broch is meticulously manicured to an almost surreal standard, yet it remains visually confusing. Looking south-south-east, we see the stump of the first century BC broch tower, originally perhaps 12 m high and surrounded by triple ditches and ramparts entered across a causeway on the east. Buildings began to fill up the space between tower and inner rampart and, over perhaps a thousand years, spread out over the defences. Abandoned while the settlement around it continued through much of the first millennium AD, the broch was robbed for building materials but retains some stone furniture and fittings, including partitions, stairs, hearths and a water-tank. These domestic details of the Iron Age are the equivalent of those three thousand years earlier at Skara Brae.

The siting of another broch on Mainland, that at Borwick near Yesnaby, appears to approach the ideal. It is on a cliff-sided peninsula above a protected landing place (foreground) with fresh water nearby. The natural strength of this position was enhanced by a wall across the landward side of the peninsula, protecting the approach to the broch tower of which the lower part on this side is visible, exposed in old excavations; but much of the equivalent portion on the seaward side has been eroded and collapsed. Occupied in the last centuries BC, the site continued into the middle of the first millennium AD. The mound to the left of the broch wall almost certainly contains a build-up of structural debris resulting from occupation over many centuries, as at Gurness; but here the site enjoys an unkempt appearance.

Midhowe broch is close to the chambered cairn of the same name on Rousay but even closer to the rocky island shore. The impressive basal remains of the tower vividly illustrate a problem and its solution which the builders and inhabitants of tall buildings can readily appreciate today. Instead of the usual solid masonry base to the broch, here the architect used a form of hollow construction by inserting a gallery into the thickness of the wall at ground level. At some stage the tower must have threatened to collapse for two strengthening devices were used. The hollow wall was partly filled in with rubble to provide it with stability; and the outside of the external skin to the wall was buttressed, as the photograph shows, by leaning a row of long flagstones against it.

(Top left) Here we look almost 10 m west-north-west across the interior of the Midhowe broch towards the lintelled doorway which gives out on to the sea and an inlet which could well have been a landing-place. A large hearth with side-sockets, presumably to support a cooking bar or even spit, water-tanks, partitions including the main one that divides the interior in half, alcoves and other details all present a convincing picture of Iron Age domestic life about the time of Christ. Conspicuously missing, however, is the ladder — presumably of wood — which would have been necessary to reach the first-floor gallery in the thickness of the wall. There is no stone-built access.

(Bottom left) So-called 'burnt mounds' feature prominently and puzzlingly in Orkney's archaeology. Here we see one at Liddle, South Ronaldsay, after excavation. A characteristic stone structure of sorts clearly exists as an irregular area defined by a built stone edge, its interior containing a stone-lined pit. Such structures are interpreted as cooking-places, sometimes open air, sometimes within buildings. The pit is believed to have held water which was heated by dropping red-hot stones into it, then used to boil meat or fish.

(Top right) Here at Rennibister, underneath the yard of a working farm on a low mound by the shore of Bay of Firth, this oval, underground chamber some 3 m long with a corbelled roof seems to be part of a late prehistoric settlement. The 'earth-house' was discovered when its roof, supported on four free-standing pillars, each one a single stone, collapsed under the weight of a threshing machine. The passage was full of domestic refuse at the time of discovery and disarticulated human bones lay on the floor.

(Bottom right) This is the inside of another earth-house on the outskirts of Kirkwall at Grain. It has been excellently preserved because its roof is 2 m below present ground level. Steps lead down to a curving passage c 5 m long and just less than a metre high; at the end is an oval chamber. The roof of both passage and chamber is of flat slabs; in the chamber itself it is, as at Rennibister, supported by four free-standing pillars. Here the view is from the entrance to the chamber, looking back towards the bottom of the steps leading to the outside. Again, the structure is likely to be part of a larger complex of buildings in use in the last centuries BC.

(Above right) Another enigmatic man-made feature of the Orkney landscape is the 'farm mound'. Examples vary considerably in extent and height and, because their contours are usually smooth, they tend to go unnoticed or be thought natural. Here, spread across the centre of the photograph and clipped by the road, is the Kirk of Howe farm mound on Papa Westray, the largest such monument on the island. Essentially this type of mound represents the accumulation of rubbish from long-lived human occupation of a particular site. It is the Orcadian equivalent of a Near Eastern tell and probably consists of midden material, accumulated in and around the remains of houses and other buildings. The growth of a mound of this size would probably have taken many hundred of years, perhaps from the later centuries BC into medieval times.

Conwy Castle overlooks the estuary of the River Conwy on the coast of North Wales. Inland, the Vale of Conwy forms a clearly defined trough in the landscape as it gradually climbs south to Betws-y-coed. On its west are the mountains of Snowdonia; on their eastern flank, overlooking the Vale to the east, lies the Maen-y-Bardd area.

It is only some 3 km long and 1 km wide, much smaller than our other three study areas, neither well known archaeologically nor much visited. It lies at *c* 350 m above sea level, so it is fairly marginal in terms of present-day habitation and farming. In fact, only one inhabited farm, Cae-coch, lies within a block of land which stretches along the contours of a south-east-facing slope above and behind Maen-y-Bardd farm itself. The whole area, with its ill-kept stone walls and bedraggled fences, looks agriculturally derelict and is now used for low-density sheep grazing. Yet this is no wilderness, if the sense of that word is remote and natural scenery unaffected by man until recent times. Despite the rough and vegetationally poor wildness of its superficial appearance, the Maen-y-Bardd area is an almost totally deserted man-made landscape of considerable antiquity and interest.

Archaeologically, in several respects Maen-y-Bardd is representative of much of upland Britain. It contains many apparently discrete sites and much of the eastern part is covered with the remains of an ancient, probably late prehistoric, enclosed landscape of stone-walled fields, settlements and lanes. Yet, while the number and variety of the archaeological features are probably typical, a special factor must be noted. A natural route through the mountains passes through the area, climbing from the valley below to the east, through the farmable zone with its present-day villages of Roewen and Llanbedr-y-cennin, to moorland and towards the pass, Bwlch-y-Ddeufaen, at 428 m above sea level. Thereafter it can drop north-westwards towards the coast between Conwy and Bangor by any one of a number of ways.

The siting of several of the prehistoric monuments hints that this route may well have been used before the Roman period; a Roman road certainly follows the line of it and is still the base for a track that runs right through the area between the pass and the Youth Hostel at Rhiw. This century, two power-lines and a gas pipe-line have all headed through that same pass, a nodal point in the landscape for at least two, maybe four, thousand years.

The Maen-y-Bardd area, looking north towards the top of Tal-y-Fan at c 600 m above sea level, clearly shows its upland nature in the wet foreground, the stone walls and rather ragged hedges, the planted tree clumps, and the treeless moorland in the distance. Many of the sites illustrated lie either side of and just beyond the clump of trees left of centre. The Bwlch-y-Ddeufaen pass is to the left, the Vale of Conwy downslope to the right, with the line of the Roman road between the two marked by a continuous, straight field wall alongside the modern track across the centre of the photograph, just behind the central tree-clump. That lies about 305 m above sea level, while the zone of surviving field archaeology rises from there to c 425 m around Caer Bach hillfort over the right shoulder of the background mountain.

Roewen East chambered cairn, here seen from the north-east, is a miniature chambered long barrow perhaps of the third millennium BC. The stones are still embedded in the remains of a mound which may originally have stretched 10 m or more to the south-west. The chamber has been disturbed and robbed without record; some damage may have been done about two thousand years ago for the cairn is within a field system of late prehistoric date. Just uphill, to the right of the photograph, are the possible remains of a settlement or further cairns. Further south-west and within the view are the Maen-y-Bardd dolmen, extreme left, and the Giant's Stick, in the rear, centre left. The stone wall between them marks the line of the Roman road. The cairn may well have existed in a contemporary enclosed landscape not entirely dissimilar to that in the background.

The Maen-y-Bardd dolmen, here viewed from the west, perhaps the only monument in the area with an archaeological reputation outside the locality, is a classic dolmen with four uprights supporting a disproportionately large capstone. Of course it did not exist in isolation; it was originally intended as a burial chamber, its entrance facing uphill, and lay at the centre of a stony mound, the remains of which are still visible. The structure, dating perhaps to c 2000 BC, is of especial interest because, like its counterparts in the Isles of Scilly, it was built on top of a field wall which runs up and down the slope to left and right of this view. Clearly the cairn was constructed within the framework of an already existing, man-made landscape. The top of the Giant's Stick is to the left, behind the modern field wall along the south side of the Roman road.

The same wall along the line of the Roman road is in the background of this view of a standing stone a short distance west of the Maen-y-Bardd dolmen. We look downslope, south-east towards Maen-y-Bardd farm with the Vale of Conwy in the background. The stone is 2.4 m high and stands on a low mound. In itself it is undated and it does not appear to be related to other features immediately around it; but it is likely to have been erected early in the second millennium BC, if not a bit earlier, and could well have been a deliberately sited part of the planned landscape hinted at by other fragments of evidence such as the dolmen in the previous photograph.

(Below) Bwlch-y-Ddeufaen, the head of the pass and the watershed, is so-named from the two standing stones upper right, the nearer c 3 m tall, the further c 2 m, here viewed from the east. Man-made features crowd together as the cross-mountain route narrows in this remote spot. In the left foreground are the ruins of the Barclodiad-y-Gawres ('The Giantess's Apronful') cairn. The monoliths may have marked a route in the second millennium BC; the gap between them is deeply worn along the line of the Roman road. The two lines of electricity pylons are themselves almost an archaeological lesson in stratigraphy in the sky with their different designs, lower and earlier on the right, higher and later on the distant left. The scattered stones on the left hillside mark a gas pipeline, a minor cause célèbre in the early seventies during the pioneering days of 'rescue' archaeology.

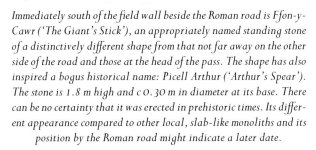

Immediately south of the field wall beside the Roman road is Ffon-y-Cawr ('The Giant's Stick'), an appropriately named standing stone of a distinctively different shape from that not far away on the other side of the road and those at the head of the pass. The shape has also inspired a bogus historical name: Picell Arthur ('Arthur's Spear'). The stone is 1.8 m high and c 0.30 m in diameter at its base. There can be no certainty that it was erected in prehistoric times. Its different appearance compared to other local, slab-like monoliths and its position by the Roman road might indicate a later date.

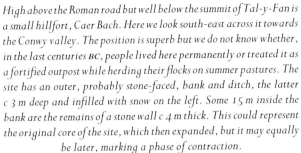

High above the Roman road but well below the summit of Tal-y-Fan is a small hillfort, Caer Bach. Here we look south-east across it towards the Conwy valley. The position is superb but we do not know whether, in the last centuries BC, people lived here permanently or treated it as a fortified outpost while herding their flocks on summer pastures. The site has an outer, probably stone-faced, bank and ditch, the latter c 3 m deep and infilled with snow on the left. Some 15 m inside the bank are the remains of a stone wall c 4 m thick. This could represent the original core of the site, which then expanded, but it may equally be later, marking a phase of contraction.

(Above) The area contains at least one stone circle, Cerrig Pryfaid. It is not particularly prominent though its site, as the photograph looking south-east across it shows, was sensitively chosen. The builders could hardly anticipate that their work would come to be sandwiched between a Roman road (to the left) and electricity power-lines. Two outlying stones lie in the foreground. The circle itself is c 20 m in diameter and contained about a dozen stones, it now being difficult to be certain of the exact number. None seem to have been of any great size or height; those visible here are knee height.

One of the characteristic forms of upland settlement in North Wales is the platform settlement, so-called because the sites were prepared by cutting back into the slope on the uphill side and piling up material on the downhill side to create an enclosed platform on which a farmstead could be built. Here is one of them, beside and possibly cut by the Roman road (this side of the field wall across the centre of the photograph). The top of 'The Giant's Stick' is visible to the south-east, above the top of the wall left of centre. The enclosure is c 26 m by 21 m and contains the sites of two or three round buildings. Two lie in the foreground at the foot of the steep, rear scarp of the enclosure. This settlement is one of several in the area apparently surrounded by a contemporary field system of the late Iron Age.

Late prehistoric fields extend across the south-facing slope above Maen-y-Bardd farm. Here we see original boundaries and a major terrace-wall against which soil has piled up, looking south-west with Roewen East chambered cairn rear right. Much of the system seems to relate to this major stone boundary running across the slope. We can see two other field walls laid off from it downslope to the left, together with small heaps of stones cleared from the field surface. The present appearance of this boundary, originally a wall, suggests that it remained a fixed line in a working landscape over a considerable period. Now but a ragged line of tumbled stones across rough pasture 335 m up a Welsh mountain, it speaks of reasonably successful farming and even of some sort of agricultural stability.

The Avebury area was undoubtedly one of the most important places in prehistoric Britain. This was especially so between 3500 and 1500 BC and, in the monuments of the area, we could be looking at the remains of a place with public functions similar to those of a city in later times.

The present landscape is of almost treeless rolling chalk downland cut by the upper reaches of the River Kennet, now a small stream which divides at Avebury. This appearance is, botanically speaking, misleading, for up to some 6000 years ago the area was forested. Thereafter, early settlers began to make clearings and, towards 3000 BC, quite extensive openings for crop cultivation and grazing along the valleys penetrating the woodland. A particular local problem seems to have been bracken infestation of the newly farmed land, some of which reverted to rough grassland and scrub in the earlier third millennium. At one site, South Street, land which had been cultivated and returned to grass was re-used for a ceremonial long mound, possibly because it had come to be regarded as worn out and agriculturally marginal. Indeed, several of the major monuments of the middle and late third millennium were built on places already with a long land-use history.

Two of the earliest visible archaeological sites lie on the northern and southern edges of the area: Windmill and Knap Hills, each with banks and ditches constructed before 3000 BC. Broadly contemporary are long mounds containing megalithic structures like the West Kennet long barrow and Adam's Grave, apparently long-lived monuments central to complex rituals associated with the disposal of the dead. Other similar mounds, like that at South Street, incorporated timberwork but had no large stones and are nowadays much less impressive. Avebury henge monument probably also began with timber structures, the full extent of its monumental and megalithic complexity only peaking towards 2000 BC. Silbury Hill, though its exact function is uncertain, can reasonably be seen as part of the same grand design.

Smaller round mounds covered burials in the cleared landscape of the second millennium BC as farms, fields, boundaries and connecting lanes developed into a countryside which, by the middle of the first millennium BC, had new focal points. Oldbury hillfort, however, like practically everything else in this ancient landscape, was probably a ruin by the time the main Roman road from Londonium to Aquae Sulis cut east—west through the area in the first century AD.

Avebury henge monument is unusually large (11.5 hectares) and unique in having four entrances. Here we look south-west at the north one, crossed on its original causeway by the modern road to Swindon. The ditch was originally as much as 10 m deep and some 21 m wide at its top; the outer bank, as much as 30 m wide at base and perhaps once up to 7 m high, is c 1350 m in circumference. These works alone could have taken $1\frac{1}{2}$ million man-hours to construct. Around the inner lip of the ditch stood the biggest prehistoric stone circle in Britain with about one hundred monoliths and a diameter of c 330 m. Relatively intact for some three thousand years, it was destroyed from the fourteenth century onwards. The stones in this view were restored after excavation in the 1930s. Beyond, where the henge bank was levelled in the seventeenth century, manorial farm buildings now provide tourist facilities in a self-consciously rustic setting. The distant tower is of St James's, a medieval adaptation of an Anglo-Saxon church.

Two avenues of standing stones approached (or led from) Avebury henge monument. Both are additions. The West Kennet Avenue connects the south entrance to 'The Sanctuary' on Overton Hill. Here, looking south away from the henge, we see it restored after excavation with concrete plinths marking the positions of missing stones. Original stones tend to be either broad and flattish, or relatively thin and rounded, the two types occurring alternately down each side of the avenue and forming dissimilar pairs across it in a clearly deliberate arrangement. Possibly the different shapes represent the idea of 'maleness' and 'femaleness', or symbolise the general concept of fecundity; but equally they might be 'petrified dancers' performing a pictorial function, perhaps of seasonal rites. We cannot ever know whether such guesses are remotely correct.

We look across the centre of the great henge monument from the top of its north bank just east of the entrance; it is c 350 m to the equivalent position on the south bank. Beyond, in the middle distance, is the stepped, cone-shaped top of Silbury Hill. Nearer, the buildings include the Red Lion at the cross-roads near the centre of the Neolithic enclosure; beside it are the two large remaining upright stones of the so-called 'Cove', built as a three-stone structure at the centre of two concentric rings of standing stones. The now-isolated stones of one stand to their left. Avebury village formerly extended along the west–east road to the Downs in front of the two houses on the left, and earthworks of this medieval occupation — such as that at the top of the inner side of the ditch in the foreground — occur over the western half of the henge.

The other Avebury avenue is well-documented but it is now represented by only one upright stone called 'Eve', here in the background to the north. 'Adam' was the east side of a separate and earlier structure, Beckhampton Cove, which was incorporated in this Beckhampton Avenue. The two stones were part of its west side as it curved south-west towards Beckhampton. Perhaps fortuitously, they appear to make a pair conforming to the pillar and diamond shapes characteristic of the stones in the West Kennet Avenue. Also known as the Devil's Quoits and the Longstones, they stand west of Avebury Trusloe village across the Kennet from Avebury village. The Avenue itself must have crossed that river as it wound its way west-wards from the west entrance of the henge monument. The West Kennet Avenue led towards the same river further south but curved away south-east towards 'The Sanctuary', passing east of an area occupied by an earlier ditched enclosure on both sides of the river.

The slight rise in the road here, and in the field on the right immediately to its north, is the last remains of the South Street long mound, built c 3500 BC and excavated in the 1960s. It was constructed in segments, divided by hurdling, on top of land which had already long been cleared, cultivated, grazed and, at one stage in the fourth millennium, fenced. The mound itself neither contained nor covered any burials; it seems to have been a ceremonial monument rather than to have had a specifically funereal function – though its purpose may have been achieved as much in its building as in its use thereafter. Ploughing came right up to the mound, crossing the silted-up ditch on its south, around 2000 BC. In the centre of the photograph, in front of the house, is another of the locally numerous burial mounds of the fourth–second millennia. Typical of this landscape too are the 200-year-old tree-clumps on the skylines of the Downs and the magnificent tree-planting around the house.

These shallow ditches are among the earliest dug in Britain as part of a planned moulding of the landscape. They lie on Windmill Hill, c 2 km north-west of Avebury. The hill is encircled by three lines of bank and ditch, each line broken by paired gaps and causeways. The three enclosures were not necessarily constructed at the same time, but the whole site was certainly in use in the centuries around 3000 BC, probably as a centre for communal, perhaps seasonal, gatherings, for both secular and ceremonial purposes. Here the view is from the bank of the outer line, south-east across one of the causeways of undug chalk bedrock, to the Kennet valley north of Avebury and the plateau of the Marlborough Downs beyond – an archetypal 'Wessex' landscape.

The best-preserved of all Neolithic causewayed enclosures lies on the top of Knap Hill overlooking the Vale of Pewsey 8 km east-south-east of Avebury. It consists of a single bank and ditch around all but the south side; it may originally have been dug there too but, if so, it has been eroded away on the steep south-facing scarp. Excavation showed the ditch to consist of a series of flat-bottomed pits 2–3 m deep separated by low baulks of undug chalk, and the bank to have been substantial, possibly even defensive in intent. Construction took place in the mid-fourth millennium but use of the site may have been short-lived. Some two thousand years later, two round barrows were also built on the hill, one inside the enclosure, the other just outside on the west-facing slope. The thin, ribbed terraces on the steep slope in the foreground are natural ledges, accentuated in some cases by sheep using them as walkways. The area, here viewed from the west, is a National Nature Reserve for its chalkland flora.

Another hilltop surrounded by prehistoric banks and ditches can be found 4.5 km west-south-west of Avebury, but here very much later than the causewayed enclosures. Rather confusingly called Oldbury Castle, the site is a hillfort of the middle centuries of the first millennium BC, not a medieval castle. It possesses particularly impressive multiple ramparts on its east, here seen looking north-west, and generally exudes an air of strength and local dominance.

Below the single rampart and ditch on the west is an eighteenth-century, chalk-cut white horse, and to the south is the Lansdowne Monument, a nineteenth-century obelisk visible from all over the Avebury area. Grandly related to the formal landscape of Bowood House 8 km to the west, it commemorates the seventeenth-century economist, Sir William Petty. The hill was acquired in 1987 by the National Trust.

Most contentious of the ceremonial sites in the Avebury area is perhaps one of the dullest-looking: 'The Sanctuary' on Overton Hill at the south-east end of the West Kennet Avenue. A pioneer archaeological excavation of 'ghost' timber structures here in 1930 exposed a complex of holes cut into the chalk; some had held wooden posts, others upright stones. Their positions are marked now by, respectively, round and rectangular concrete blocks. They represent at least three main phases: a small round timber building; a larger one, probably roofed; and a stone circle, finally of two concentric rings, still standing in 1670 when seen by John Aubrey, but recorded by Stukeley as destroyed some fifty years later. Thus the medley of concrete on Overton Hill, itself a monument to good intentions in the 1930s, represents a ceremonial monument that probably began soon after c 3000 BC, centuries before the first structures at Avebury, and developed over perhaps a thousand years, during which time Silbury Hill and the West Kennet Avenue were built. Later, its sanctity as a stone circle perhaps still respected, it became the focus of a cluster of round burial mounds.

(Opposite page) The siting of 'The Sanctuary' is sensitive, overlooking the River Kennet and, beyond, the East Kennet long barrow, now marked by an isolated tree-clump. But perhaps, rather than look out from 'The Sanctuary', we should think of what was meant to be looked at from the valley below and the Downs beyond. Certainly many of the Avebury monuments are placed on higher ground apparently for visibility from the valley-bottom locations of Avebury henge, the Avenues, and Silbury Hill. The East Kennet long barrow is a good example in this respect, the view from its site looking north-east across to 'The Sanctuary' and down on Silbury Hill. In what was conceivably a 'landscape of ancestors' it is also prominent looked at from below, from land where much scattered evidence suggests people were living during the later fourth and third millennia. East Kennet long barrow itself, an unexcavated mound with, probably, an entrance and burial chambers at its higher, southern end and ditches along its sides, is 105 m long, 30 m wide and up to 6 m high. With its counterpart at West Kennet, it is one of the two largest megalithic tombs in southern England.

Adam's Grave, another chambered long barrow, stands on the Pewsey Vale escarpment 3.5 km south of Avebury. It is 60 m long and some 6 m high at its higher, south-eastern end where sarsen stones are exposed. With Knap Hill causewayed enclosure to the south-east, it forms a visually impressive twosome, possibly one of the very earliest examples of landscape architecture in the sense of the deliberate creation of a striking effect by the combination of manmade and natural structures. Between them is the Ridgeway route along which sarsen stones were perhaps hauled from the Marlborough Downs towards Stonehenge over 4000 years ago. Relatively recent but now abandoned tracks and terraces of this ancient route scar the hillside in the foreground and away to the left. Over the skyline is another 'white horse', cut in 1812 and copying the one below Oldbury hillfort.

West Kennet chambered long barrow is also delicately sited. Its great mound, 100 m long, almost 3 m high at its east end, and originally flanked by side ditches 3 m deep and 6 m wide some 10 m out from its base, stretches along the top of a swell in the rolling downland. Best known of the tombs in the Avebury area, it has been excavated and consolidated, and is accessible on foot from the A4. The approaching visitor is presented with this view from the north. The entrance to the central passage and burial chambers is under the higher end to the left where the profile of the restored blocking stone is silhouetted. The hummocks in the centre of the profile result from quarrying but further right the spine of the mound slopes away in the classic fashion of its type to a point which provides a direct line of view to Silbury Hill, with Windmill Hill behind.

In this view of Overton Hill along the A4 from the east, 'The Sanctuary' stood just over the skyline to the left of the road; any upper structure, such as a roof, would have been visible from here in the valley if the landscape was as treeless in the third millennium BC as now. The later round barrows to the right are not, despite appearances, on the top of the ridge either; rather they are sensitively placed along a false crest to appear on the skyline when viewed from below, so reinforcing our belief that the landscape by the early second millennium was largely treeless. The mounds visible here are only part of a larger cemetery now much reduced by cultivation. The modern clutter on the skyline behind the barrows includes a transport cafe, the site in 1988 of a proposed multi-conical hotel, in design supposedly sympathetic to the barrow shapes. The proposal was rejected after a public inquiry; now the excrescences have been removed by the new owner, the National Trust.

Despite its position down in the Kennet valley, Silbury Hill somehow visually dominates the Avebury area. It seems to lurk on the lower ground, appearing unexpectedly in other views, for example when looking round the south side of Waden Hill up the Kennet valley from 'The Sanctuary', across Avebury itself from its northern bank, and from the Ridgeway, 2 km east, whence just the top suddenly appears at certain points. Here it sits pudding-like, seen from the West Kennet long barrow looking north with Windmill Hill in the background. It is sited on the end of a spur of chalk, here dropping from the left, cut by a huge ditch.

Some 40 m high, Silbury Hill's level top is c 30 m in diameter above a base covering just over 2 hectares, giving a volume of rather more than a quarter of a million cubic metres constructed in perhaps something of the order of 18 million man-hours. The resultant symmetry, horizontality and stability of the largest man-made mound in prehistoric Europe make it an unprecedented and unique monumental achievement.

This classic dolmen is both part of a genuine prehistoric monument and a modern botch-up. Devil's Den, a name itself redolent of rustic explanation, is the remains of a Neolithic chambered long barrow like West Kennet. It occupies the floor of a dry combe called Clatford Bottom 5.5 km east of Avebury. Its mound was gradually reduced by cultivation, leaving the remains of the stone structure at its east end as an apparently distinct megalithic dolmen. After sundry inadequate excavations, in 1921 the megaliths were restored, creating this visually attractive but scientifically silly monument conforming to an already archaic stereotype.

Stoney Valley, 3 km east of Avebury, preserves the sort of landscape from which sarsen stones for megalithic structures were dragged; some may indeed have come from here. These blocks of tabular sandstone reputedly made it possible to walk from Avebury to Marlborough without touching the ground. The largest surviving stone (upper right centre) points up the one natural way out of the combe towards Avebury; it was perhaps abandoned there soon after starting a long haul to a henge. The stone in the foreground was split during small-scale quarrying practised here until 1939.

This is the surviving part of a sarsen stone which was split, probably early in the thirteenth century when a halfpenny of King John was lost beside it. The right-hand edge shows indentations where iron wedges were driven in; one such wedge, exactly fitting the wedge-marks, was also left behind. The smoothed and hardened surface glistens because, about 3000 years earlier, harder stones were polished on it, stones of metamorphic rocks from west and north Britain. The clutch of grooves represents countless hours spent sharpening the edges of implements made of such rocks. In other words, this remarkable stone on Overton Down, 3 km east of Avebury, is a Neolithic work-bench of the type that produced some of those beautifully finished stone axes in the museums of Avebury, Devizes and Salisbury.

(Opposite page) A low bank and slight ditch run down the slope through the gorse, across a shallow valley, and up the facing slope towards the copse on the skyline. The area left of the bank and ditch is archaeologically blank but, to their right, many slight earthworks demonstrate that here, on clay-with-lints overlying chalk subsoil at c 225 m above sea level, farmers grew crops in field systems which occupied the same patch of land in the second millennium BC, in the first millennium BC, and in the early Roman period. The linear bank and ditch formed a major land division in the first of those phases; in the last, over a thousand years later, in its silted-up state, the ditch was used as a farm track. No cultivation has taken place here since c 100 AD. Now, the invading hawthorn, gorse, nettles and thistles give an impression of what undergrazed or abandoned farmlands could have looked like at any time in the Avebury area over the last four thousand years.

Cornwall is a long county, stretching far out into the Atlantic Ocean and across the sea routes north and south along the western edges of Europe. Its furthest tip in English terms – but the nearest landfall if you are coming in from the Atlantic – is topographically almost separated from the mainland by an isthmus, an area of low-lying land striking diagonally south-south-west from the mouth of the River Hayle, then inland up its valley across to Marazion and St Michael's Mount. It is the remote and rocky area west of this divide that is West Penwith, an area completely surrounded by sea except for the land-divide on its east.

Archaeologically, West Penwith is of considerable importance. Its field archaeology reflects in marked fashion the local geology, the geographical and cultural position of the peninsula, and the land-use there over at least the last three thousand years. Much of the present working landscape, especially of the higher, granite plateaux stretched at c 150 m or more above sea level across the northern half of West Penwith, is deeply enmeshed in the functions, structures and patterns of much older countrysides developed in the second and first millennia AD. And, unlike much of the rest of England, the structural impact of Roman imperialism on an already old landscape seems to have been slight at this westernmost extremity of Rome's westernmost province. Novel varieties of land organisation and settlement pattern did not break or significantly interrupt the prehistoric way of life. Later, it was the adoption of Celtic Christianity rather than the early imposition of Anglo-Saxon hegemony which added a new layer to a landscape which, stripped of its post-medieval industrial workings and present tourist tawdrinesses in places such as Land's End, remains recognisably ancient.

In part this visual impression stems from the superabundance of stone and particularly of granite. The bedrock of much of the area is granite; its weathering over millennia littered the landscape with boulders and, where man would farm, he had to clear them. Some areas are still uncleared today but where man has worked, the fundamentally megalithic nature of his boundaries around fields and along lanes has tended to keep prehistoric landscape patterns in place. Successors had neither the incentive nor the power to move them, at least until recently when much of this old landscape has been destroyed or threatened by the application of mechanical power. Similarly many of the prehistoric structures, especially houses, farmsteads and places of the dead, were also built, at least in part, of granite boulders. They too, even when abandoned, have tended to survive. As a result, despite the thin soils, despite the difficulty that vegetation has to establish itself here, despite the erosion, the wind and the rain on what is in effect England's exposed southwestern headland, archaeology has done well in West Penwith.

The understanding of this archaeology intellectually, in parallel with the recording of it physically, has been advanced over two centuries by a distinguished line of scholars. This brief case study can accordingly do little more than nod in the direction of an extensive survival of old landscapes, a multitude of prehistoric sites and a plenitude of ideas.

West Penwith contains examples of a variety of archaeological sites, surviving as visible structures dating from the fourth millennium right through to 'native' settlements occupied in the Roman period. There are many, many more than the selection here might suggest, though we have chosen carefully to exemplify the variety. One of the attractions of the area is that most of the sites can be visited with little difficulty. If the site is not obviously open to the public as a National Trust site or an English Heritage property, a modicum of courtesy to a nearby farmer and a little walking along a track or across some moorland usually brings you to a recognisably ancient structure.

The fact that no-one else may be there should not blind a visitor to the intense local interest in the monuments and the considerable lore about them. Compared to many interpretations, including some in print, of the 'ancient stones' of the area, ours is a very sober account; but we are nevertheless very conscious of following an honoured tradition of painters, poets, writers, visionaries, scholars and photographers, all with their own images to create and convey, in looking at antiquity in the landscapes of West Penwith.

Cliffs and granite dominate not just the scenery but also the archaeology of West Penwith. The sea, often dangerous, and the rocky coast with its few safe harbours and long history of shipwreck, are crucial to appreciation of life in West Penwith. The cliff-tops carry an impressive array of archaeological sites. Gurnard's Head, the longest promontory on the north coast west of St Ives, was demarcated on its southern, landward side in the last centuries before Christ by three ramparts and ditches looped across its neck. Their precise position at the bottom of the slope dropping from the higher cliff-land to their south (upper centre left) is not tactically ideal in military terms. The apparently modern fields (top left), now partly abandoned, are defined by scarps resulting from long-lived cultivation. Very probably, they perpetuate much older land boundaries.

(Below) Bosporthennis farm between Zennor and Morvah on the
north coast has recently been acquired by the National Trust in large
part for its archaeological interest — not so much because it is a
conventional archaeological site but because it is an ancient landscape, by accident extremely well preserved. In all probability, the
basic arrangement of fields, tracks and settlements is essentially
that of two thousand and more years ago. The standing buildings
are, of course, later but the small, irregular, stone-walled fields
and the wobbly, double-walled lane winding between them seem to
represent a prehistoric patchwork resulting from clearance of this
boulder-strewn land by early farmers.

(Above right) Looking east-north-east towards England from West
Penwith's highest eastern point in the late-prehistoric Trencrom
hillfort south of St Ives, we see the wide sweep of St Ives Bay curving
past Hayle to Godrevy Towans and the distant heights of St Agnes
Head. Inland lies the relatively fertile plateau around
Camborne/Redruth, notable for its archaeology, local history and
former mining wealth. The hill extreme right is Carn Brea, marked
by its obelisk. People have lived on the area of sand-dunes (left)
around Godrevy and the Red River estuary since Mesolithic times.
Godrevy Island off it, with its picturesque lighthouse, has inspired
many a painter, as well as Virginia Woolf's 'To the Lighthouse'.
Trencrom's eastern entrance is in the foreground.

Hillforts overlook the ancient landscapes of West Cornwall. Chun
Castle south of Morvah is one with fine views over the coastal plateau
and along the north coast. It has complex defences, and the ruins
represent several phases of occupation, covering perhaps a thousand
years up to the fifth–sixth centuries AD. Here the view is from the west
side, looking inwards at the west entrance. Breaking the skyline are
the gateposts of the entrance through the inner rampart, marked by
piles of boulders to left and right.

(Left) In the corner of a stone-walled field near Bosporthennis is a remarkable round building of unmortared granite, virtually complete except for its roof, originally a corbelled structure. The interior was entered from the right through the doorway with its lintel still in position. A small recessed room to the left is characteristic of local Iron Age houses, and a stone cupboard in the centre contains, presumably symbolically for some latter-day pagan, a lump of quartz within a circlet of plaited grass.

(Above) The 'fogou' on the northern coastal plateau at Pendeen House is in a farmyard, its above-ground structure damaged and its collapsed original entrance in the field beyond. Entry is now through a black opening at muck level into the impressive stone-built passage and chamber, an example of an underground structure typical of the late prehistoric settlements in West Penwith. It could have been used for storage, animals, protection or ritual.

The view south-west along a fogou at Carn Euny, a rural settlement occupied more or less continuously from the late fifth century BC into the fourth century AD, shows the passage, 1.8 m high and 20 m long. There is a 'creep' on the right.

199

(Below) At Carn Euny, inside an underground corbelled chamber built into a pit cut 2.5 m into the bedrock, we look through its low, lintelled entrance into a 1.37 m high passage which slopes up to connect with the fogou beyond in a complex of stone structures. These were in use from the fourth–third centuries BC. In the foreground is a rubbing stone on a horizontal, dished stone used for grinding.

(Above right) Chysauster village, some 4 km north of Penzance, consists of eight so-called courtyard houses on each side of a common road. Each house contains a central space, originally open, surrounded by a number of 'rooms' in the thickness of the courtyard wall. These outer rooms, roofed and sometimes drained, were lived in and perhaps used for animals. This view shows one house with its central courtyard, surrounding rooms and a side road to the left.

Four of the houses at Chysauster are visible here from the edge of a side road between two houses. The main street runs from left to right at right angles and in front of two further houses, each an individually compact unit protected by thick walls and narrow, passage-like entrances. Two of the latter can be seen on houses 6 (centre), the back entrance from the outside, and 5 (centre right), the front entrance from the inside.

The Pipers, near Boleigh on the south of the Land's End peninsula, are two unusually tall standing stones of granite, now separated by a hedge. The further one to the north-east is c 5 m high with another 1.5 m buried in the ground; the nearer one is not quite as tall. If projected to the south-west, a line through them would touch the edge of the Merry Maidens stone circle c 350 m to the south-west, though the two sites, presumably interrelated, are not intervisible. Another part of the arrangement could be Goon Rith, a menhir or standing stone about the same distance west of the Merry Maidens.

The Merry Maidens, as perfect a circle of standing stones as Victorian restoration achieved anywhere, number nineteen and stand some 350 m south-west of the Pipers. Here they are viewed from the south-east with St Buryan church tower on the skyline. The circle they form is 23.8 m in diameter with a possible entrance on the north-east. Actually about four thousand years old, the stones have been explained since at least the early eighteenth century as petrified dancers punished for dancing on the Sabbath, the story nicely illustrating the application of Christian morality to a prehistoric, pagan monument.

Another stone circle, this time of Nine Maidens, near Tregeseal a little to the north of St Just near the west coast, is here viewed looking north-east towards Carn Kenidjack, a natural granite outcrop on open moorland marked by several burial mounds. It was one of a pair, its western counterpart having been virtually destroyed. This one contains re-erected stones. It was also seriously damaged internally in the 1980s by badly misguided treasure-hunters fruitlessly and illegally hacking up the ground as they quested a Great Golden Egg, a stunt dreamed up by a well-known firm of chocolate purveyors.

On the north coast east of Morvah, the unusual line of standing stones called Men-an-Tol consists of a fallen stone and two terminal stones, perhaps not now in their original positions, bracketing a central one 1.11 m high with a hole through its middle. The arrangement of the three stones may have been triangular but we can still only guess at the original purpose and a date early in the second millennium BC. Again folklore, and particularly folk-practice, might conceivably contain a hint of former beliefs. The holed stone, known in the nineteenth century as the Devil's Eye, has also been called the Crick Stone for its supposed power to cure 'crick in the neck' (rickets) in children who were passed three or nine times through the hole towards the sun, from woman to a man if a boy and from man to a woman if a girl. The stone had other curative properties too and is a particularly well-documented example of the attribution in recent centuries of healing powers to a prehistoric stone monument.

Pennance entrance grave, here seen looking north-west towards Gurnard's Head, lies on sloping agricultural land. It exemplifies a type of small megalithic tomb peculiar to West Penwith and the Isles of Scilly characterised by a round mound kerbed with upright stones, an entrance, and an elongated and lintelled central chamber. Now damaged and only 1.5 m high, with its collapsed entrance to the right, its appearance and siting typify a class of local monument which, in 1865, was first recognised here.

One of the largest barrows in West Penwith, Carn Gluze or Gloose, alternatively the Ballowal Barrow, lies near the cliff-edge beside a minor road from St Just. It looks an extraordinary sight from the road but from the cliff-edge it is more recognisably a large round cairn, probably of the early second millennium BC. Nevertheless, its disturbance by mining, its uncomprehending excavation in 1878–9 and its subsequent 'restoration' make interpretation difficult, particularly as the most obvious features, this northern entrance and the main inner wall, are Victorian. A primary stone mound encircled by a double-faced drystone wall covered three cist-graves. Against it, on south-west and north-east, two further cists were built. Subsequently all this was covered by a kerbed stone mound c 21 m in diameter into which an entrance grave was built on the south-west in line with the other burials.

Bosiliack cairn is a miniature version of Carn Gluze. In a sense it is the most recent addition to the antiquities of West Penwith for, although it was originally built c 1500 BC, it was recently excavated, found to be in an undisturbed state, and has been left exposed after modest 'restoration' for anybody to see. Here viewed from the south-south-east, its two upright entrance pillars stand flanking the blocked entrance into a short, simple chamber, terminated at the far end by the tallest upright stone in the structure. In the chamber was a primary cremation burial partly in and partly round a pottery urn. The mound was of stones, retained by a circle of upright granite blocks. Situated inconspicuously in typical granite landscape of unenclosed moorland, the site is accessible on foot close to a right of way uphill from Lanyon Quoit and a few hundred metres south-west of the euphoniously named Ding Dong mine.

(Opposite page) Lanyon Quoit is the best known of West Penwith's archaeological sites. Despite its supposed mysteriousness and visual impressiveness, the Quoit is but the remains, re-erected in 1824, of a burial chamber originally encased in a mound, built c 2000 BC and subsequently quarried away. With its two portal stones to the left and the single terminal stone to the right, this monument can be interpreted as a larger version, but with its capstone in position, of the Bosiliack burial chamber up the hill.

(Left) Chun Quoit lies isolated on open moorland some 300 m from the west entrance to Chun Castle. Overlooking the north coast of West Penwith, here seen from its south, again the romantically named Quoit is more prosaically the central burial chamber of a probably kerbed cairn dating to c 3000 BC. Traces of the round cairn remain but in this case its diameter of only c 12 m suggests that the large capstone may originally have been visible. The Quoit itself consists of four uprights supporting the capstone, a granite slab almost 4 m square, the whole structure in effect making a closed box. It was possibly approached by an inturned entrance through the mound from the south-east. Such an explanation in no way conveys the sense of desolate grandeur invoked for many by this site and its situation, or indeed by many of the other monuments, whether illustrated here or not, on the granite uplands of West Penwith.

IMAGES OF PREHISTORY

The hardware of prehistory exists in the landscape and in museums. The idea of prehistory exists primarily in our minds, with books and various other media recording our thoughts and attempting to convey to others what we think. This very act of communication is part of the dynamic of the prehistoric past for our thought may be changed in someone else's understanding and be changed again by someone else's reaction to it. The monuments in the landscape, the materials in museums may stay the same but the dialogue we engage in about them constantly changes. For this reason, it is dangerous, for example, to write a book about prehistory for even if it is up to date when written it will almost certainly be out of date when published. Paradoxically, in the world of learning, the act of creation by its nature is also an act of fossilisation. This applies to all attempts to recreate the past, and especially to those involving structures, ranging from the most conservative of physical restorations to the wild gymnastics of contemporary paganism.

At the simplest level, we often try to reconstruct what our predecessors saw, though of course what we actually see is at best what we think they might have seen, and probably only part of the whole anyway. West Kennet long barrow, easily accessible and visited by thousands of people every year, takes its place in the story and the landscape of the Avebury area. Yet its present appearance is very much the product of the passage of time and of various interventions by people with differing intentions and different images of what they were dealing with. As it stands now, the long barrow is not physically how a Neolithic person would have seen it; and even if it was, he or she would have seen it differently from us psychologically. We know that what is seen depends crucially on the standpoint of the observer from the wildly different depictions of the same monument, such as Avebury and Stonehenge, made over the last few centuries by antiquaries and other visitors. At the very least such different perceptions are likely to have existed much longer ago.

In going to one of the monuments of the sort illustrated in this book we cannot hope, therefore, to visit the past in any rational sense. Even a well-preserved monument will be flawed in some way: either restoration will be wrong or overdone or tasteless, as with the lavatorial bottle-glass in the chamber roof at West Kennet; and if overgrown and unrestored, the remains will be superficially meaningless however precious their scientific potential.

This view of the east end of the West Kennet long barrow, Avebury, Wiltshire, is entirely a modern creation. We look through what would have been empty space in the forecourt in front of the passage entrance while the barrow was open c 3000 BC and before the large stones on the right were erected; and also through what would have been a solid mass of rubble after the passage was extended to the line of the façade and eventually blocked by the huge central sarsen. Neither the view nor this way into the central passage existed until 1956 when both were created through meticulous restoration following detailed excavation. The result is a much more readily accessible and understandable monument, authentic but curiously unreal. Ironically, while a monumental impressiveness has been recreated for the modern visitor by restoring the façade, this end of the barrow was originally made to look like this specifically to stop people entering.

This prehistoric interior was created in the 1970s at Butser Ancient Farm in the Queen Elizabeth Country Park, near Petersfield, Hampshire. Based on a pattern of chalk-cut post-holes excavated on an Iron Age settlement at Pimperne in Dorset, the large round house was constructed partly for experimental and educational reasons, partly as the central showpiece for fee-paying visitors. Structurally, to span c 30 m diameter of a round timber building without a central post by using a ring beam supported on an aisle of shorter uprights was in itself quite a challenge. The fittings are all modern but reasonably realistic. The whole, especially in its massive statement about organic materials, emphasises the extent to which excavated evidence is defective. It creates its own credible, but uncheckable, atmosphere.

One way of sidestepping the problem is to make a substitute for the reality or, more correctly, for what we imagine the reality to have been. By setting out to recreate some imagined reality, however, it is so easy to end up creating something which has a reality, or at least a credibility, of its own, a quality which may or may not mirror the reality originally in mind, never mind the actual reality that once existed. Thus the huge Iron Age house at Butser, impressive in its own right and a magnificent achievement of the 1970s, is at least three stages removed from the original reality of c 300 BC. Its interior *may* look very different from that of the house on which it is modelled but, for various reasons, the disparity is unlikely to be great; in any case, this modern creation has a credibility of its own which makes us *think* that this is what the interior of an Iron Age house could, perhaps even would, have been like. Certainly this structure invites participation, intellectually and through the imagination, for it presents a challenge about which it is difficult to be neutral. Its construction, unlike so many so-called historic and ancient reconstructions today, is based on good archaeological evidence, scrupulously assessed and thoughtfully translated into three-dimensional form. But the building remains first and foremost a modern idea expressed in full-scale, physical form.

Re-creation, image-building, is a rather different matter when it involves the original site, already some 2000 years or more old and, so many would argue, to be respected for that reason alone. If a structure has survived as long as that, who are we to damage it? Does it not deserve to survive for struggling through so much? These are strong arguments, though by no means always strong enough to prevent damage, not least from those for whom increasing age means increasing irrelevance rather than growing respect. Yet nowadays even respect is not enough, at least in the sense that it has hitherto led to a sort of preservation that has set the monument aside as a curio, something to be looked at but not used. The whole thrust of the Ancient Monuments Acts over a century up to 1983 was to this effect.

No longer is this so. On the one hand the institutional guardians of the heritage now make positive use of some of the sites in their care by promoting events at them, both spurious and otherwise. On the other hand, and probably of greater intellectual interest, a small but growing number of people seek to use some sites, especially prehistoric ones with an air of mystery about them, for what they regard as religious

purposes. Stonehenge is the most highly publicised example but numerous other sites are also now involved. The most significant point here is that archaeological sites are perceived by those wanting to use them in this way not as defunct structures only of interest to scholars and tourists, but as live sites functioning in contemporary, late-twentieth-century society. Others may scorn the ideology or just deplore a seemingly bogus religious use as demeaning or, perhaps even damaging to, the monument. Nevertheless, it seems fitting to end with a prehistoric monument very much in contemporary use for purposes which might conceivably relate in some way to those of two thousand years ago. A Cornish fogou, dark, damp and dangerous from one point of view, is a place of worship from another. It may be so many metres long, wide and high, it may be built in interesting ways, but it is also a place of powerful symbolism, secret, tomb-like, sexual, and fecund. However questionable its present use by rational criteria, the recreation involved is doubtless very 'real' to those who now use it as a shrine. This underground, man-made cave, slightly chill yet apparently touched with innocence in its candle-lit silence, seems strangely pathetic as a very particular image of prehistory.

Modern candles for present-day religious purposes flicker in the darkness of the genuinely prehistoric Boleigh fogou buried in the grounds of a house tucked away in deepest Cornwall, now open as the Centre for Alternative Education and Research. The structure is within a hillfort and not far to the west are The Pipers standing stones and the Merry Maidens stone circle — so, for the receptive, the area is fairly numinous. The shrine-like nature of the fougou in its present guise is enhanced by the deliberately placed fir-cone in a crevice of the left-hand wall and by the flowers on the floor, bottom right. Doubtless meaningful to those involved, is this, one wonders, symptomatic of soft-centred nonsense or closer in fact to the spirit of prehistory than hard-core, scientific archaeology can ever obtain?

(Opposite page) The tree-shrouded profile of Chanctonbury Ring hillfort on the Sussex Downs, seen from the east near Wiston Park, West Sussex. Inside slight earthwork defences lies a pagan temple of the Roman period.

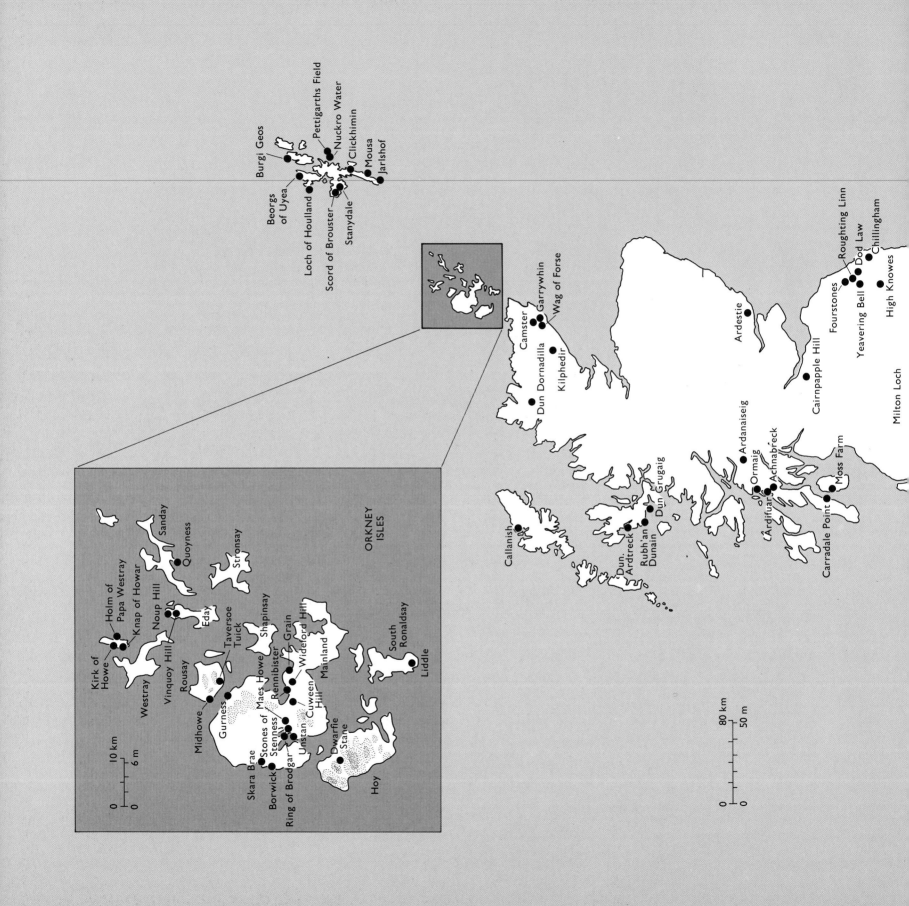

Burgi Geos
Beorgs of Uyea
Loch of Houlland
Scord of Brouster
Stanydale
Pettigarths Field
Nuckro Water
Clickhimin
Mousa
Jarlshof

ORKNEY ISLES

Sanday
Quoyness
Holm of Papa Westray
Knap of Howar
Kirk of Howe
Noup Hill
Vinquoy Hill
Westray
Rousay
Eday
Stronsay
Shapinsay
Taversoe Tuick
Midhowe
Gurness
Rennibister
Grain
Wideford Hill
Mainland
Cuween Hill
Skara Brae
Stones of Stenness
Maes Howe
Borwick
Ring of Brodgar
Unstan
Dwarfie Stane
Hoy
South Ronaldsay
Liddle

10 km
6 m
0

Camster
Garrywhin
Wag of Forse
Dun Dornadilla
Kilphedir

Ardestie

Fourstones
Roughting Linn
Dod Law
Chillingham
Yeavering Bell
High Knowes
Cairnpapple Hill
Milton Loch

Callanish

Ardanaiseig
Ormaig
Ardifuar
Achnabreck
Dun Ardtreck
Rubh'an Dunain
Dun Grugaig
Carradale Point
Moss Farm

80 km
50 m
0

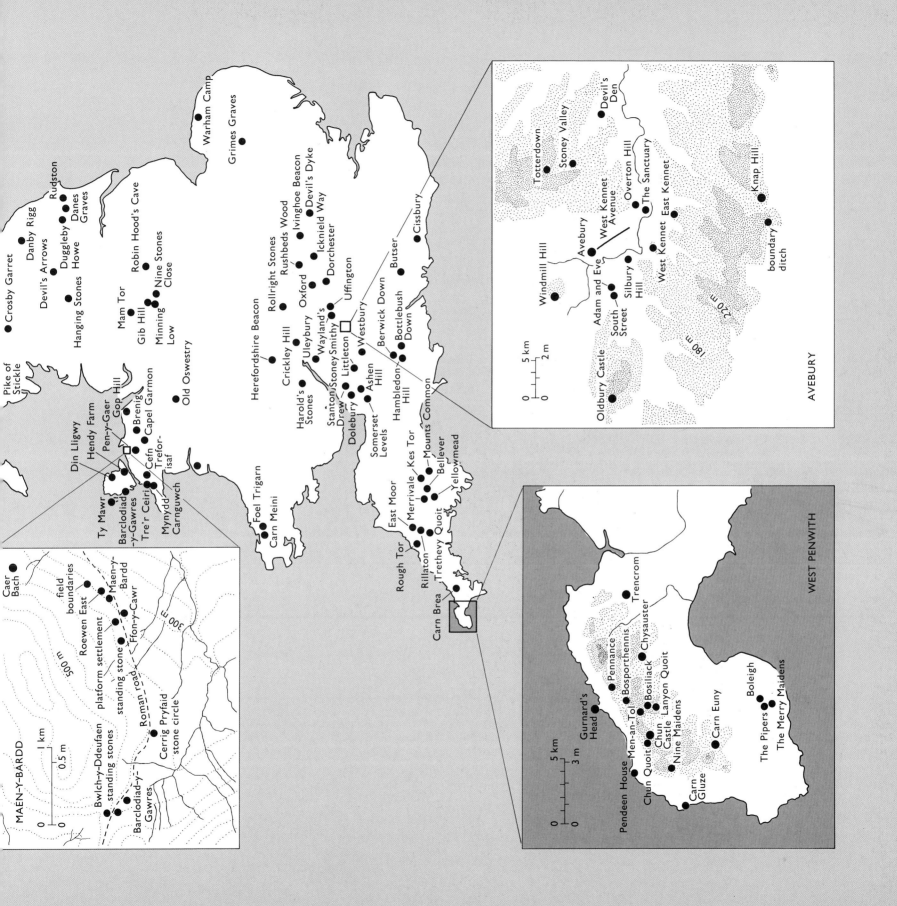

Warham Camp
Grimes Graves

Crosby Garret
Danby Rigg
Devil's Arrows
Duggleby Howe
Danes Graves
Rudston
Hanging Stones
Mam Tor
Gib Hill
Robin Hood's Cave
Nine Stones Close
Minning Low
Old Oswestry

Pike of Stickle
Din Lligwy
Hendy Farm
Pen-y-Gaer
Gop Hill
Brenig
Capel Garmon
Cefn
Trefor-isaf
Ty Mawr
Barclodiad-y-Gawres
Tre'r Ceiri
Mynydd Carnguwch

Foel Trigarn
Carn Meini

Herefordshire Beacon
Crickley Hill
Harold's Stones
Stanton Drew
Dolebury
Somerset Levels
Rough Tor
Rillaton
Carn Brea

Rollright Stones
Rushbeds Wood
Ivinghoe Beacon
Devil's Dyke
Icknield Way
Dorchester
Uffington
Uleybury
Oxford
Wayland's Smithy
Littleton
Westbury
Ashen Hill
Hambledon Hill
Berwick Down
Bottlebush Down
Butser
Cissbury
Mounts Common
Bellever
Yellowmead
East Moor
Merrivale
Kes Tor
Tretheve Quoit

MAEN-Y-BARDD

Caer'r Bach
field boundaries
Roewen East
Maen-y-Bardd
platform settlement
Ffon-y-Cawr
standing stone
Roman road
Bwlch-y-Ddeufaen standing stones
Cerrig Pryfaid stone circle
Barclodiad-y-Gawres
1 km
0.5 m
300 m
500 m
0
0

AVEBURY

Totterdown
Stoney Valley
Devil's Den
Overton Hill
West Kennet Avenue
The Sanctuary
Knap Hill
Windmill Hill
Avebury
Adam and Eve
South Street
Silbury Hill
West Kennet
East Kennet
Oldbury Castle
boundary ditch
220 m
180 m
5 km
2 m
0
0

WEST PENWITH

Trencrom
Pennance
Bosporthennis
Chysauster
Gurnard's Head
Men-an-Tol
Bosiliack
Lanyon Quoit
Carn Euny
Boleigh
Pendeen House
Chun Quoit
Chun Castle
Nine Maidens
Carn Gluze
The Pipers
The Merry Maidens
5 km
3 m
0
0

Ashbee, Paul. *The Bronze Age Round Barrow in Britain*, Phoenix, 1960

Ashbee, Paul. *The Earthen Long Barrow in Britain*, Geo Books, 1984

Aubrey, John. *Monumenta Britannica*, Dorset Publishing Co., 1980

Barnatt, John. *Prehistoric Cornwall, The Ceremonial Monuments*, Turnstone, 1982

Beckensall, Stan. *Rock Carvings of Northern Britain*, Shire, 1986

Bradley, Richard. *The Prehistoric Settlement of Britain*, Routledge & Kegan Paul, 1978

Burl, Aubrey. *Prehistoric Avebury*, Yale University Press, 1979

Burl, Aubrey. *The Stone Circles of the British Isles*, Yale University Press, 1976

Coles, Bryony and John. *Sweet Track to Glastonbury – The Somerset Levels in Prehistory*, Thames and Hudson, 1986

Darvill, Tim. *Prehistoric Britain*, Batsford, 1987

Darvill, Tim. *The Archaeology of the Uplands*, Council for British Archaeology, 1986

Dyer, James. *The Penguin Guide to Prehistoric England and Wales*, 1981

Feachem, Richard W. *A Guide to Prehistoric Scotland*, Batsford, 1976

Fenton, Alexander. *The Northern Isles: Orkney and Shetland*, John Donald, 1978

Fleming, Andrew. *The Dartmoor Reaves*, Batsford, 1988

Fowler, Peter. *The Farming of Prehistoric Britain*, Cambridge University Press, 1983

Grinsell, Leslie. *Folklore of Prehistoric Sites in Britain*, David and Charles, 1976

Hogg, Alexander. *Hill-Forts of Britain*, Granada, 1975

Houlder, Christopher. *Wales: an Archaeological Guide*, Faber, 1978

Jones, Martin. *England before Domesday*, Batsford, 1986

Marples, Morris. *White Horses and Other Hill Figures*, Alan Sutton, 1981

Marwick, Ernest. *The Folklore of Orkney and Shetland*, Batsford, 1986

Morrison, Iain. *Landscape with Lake Dwellings. The Crannogs of Scotland*, Edinburgh University Press, 1985

Muir, Richard and Welfare, Humphrey. *The National Trust Guide to Prehistoric and Roman Britain*, George Philip, 1983

Ordnance Survey *Ancient Britain*, 1982

Renfrew, Colin. (ed.) *British Prehistory – A New Outline*, Duckworth, 1974

Renfrew, Colin. (ed.) *The Prehistory of Orkney, Edinburgh University Press, 1985*

Reynolds, Peter. *Iron-Age Farm: The Butser Experiment*, British Museum, 1979

Ritchie, Anna and Graham. *The Ancient Monuments of Orkney*, HMSO, 1986

Ritchie, Anna and Graham. *Scotland, Archaeology and Early History*, Thames and Hudson, 1985

Royal Commission on Ancient and Historical Monuments in Wales
Inventory . . . Anglesey, HMSO, 1937
Inventory . . . Caernarvonshire I-III, HMSO, 1956–64

Royal Commission on the Ancient and Historical Monuments of Scotland
Exploring Scotland's Heritage (eight books covering the whole of Scotland), HMSO, 1985–7

Stanford, Stan. *The Archaeology of the Welsh Marches*, Collins, 1980

Thom, Alexander. *Megalithic Sites in Britain*, Oxford University Press, 1967

Thomas, Nicholas. *Guide to Prehistoric England*, Batsford, 1976

Todd, Malcolm. *The South-West to* AD 1000, Longman, 1987

Westwood, Jennifer. *Albion, A Guide to Legendary Britain*, Paladin, 1987

ACKNOWLEDGEMENTS

We would both like to thank the many dozens of people in England, Scotland and Wales who made our photography and fieldwork possible by allowing us on to their property. We received not one single refusal and countless kindnesses. We benefited from a generally helpful response by the main institutional site owners, English Heritage, Historic Buildings and Monuments, Scottish Development Department, Cadw, and the National Trust for England and Wales, and would express our gratitude in particular to Steven Andrews and Louise Twigs (English Heritage), Jenny Hess (HBM/SDD) and Andrew Lewis (Cadw). On specific sites, we owe a lot to Val Lord and Don Moor (Grimes Graves) and the custodians at Chysauster, Jarlshof, Maes Howe and Skara Brae; Jo May at Boleigh, Peter Reynolds at Butser and Gill Swanton at Overton Down were also particularly helpful. It was thanks to the park warden that we were able to photograph the Chillingham wild white cattle, and the Dowager Countess of Tankerville gave permission to reproduce a plate here. We are also happy to acknowledge the permission of the Cambridge University Committee on Aerial Photography to reproduce the three photographs on pp. 13, 14 and 15. Advice and practical help, especially in the form of accommodation for Mick Sharp over many years, has come from lots of friends, some of them professional colleagues. There are too many to mention them all by name unfortunately, but we would like to acknowledge the specific help towards this book received from Priscilla Boniface and Dr C.A. Smith (Department of Archaeology, University of Newcastle upon Tyne), Brigid Fowler (St Anne's College, Oxford), Nicholas Johnson (Cornwall Archaeological Unit), Professor Charles Thomas (Institute of Cornish Studies), Dave Thompson (Gwynedd Archaeological Trust), and the University of Newcastle upon Tyne Research (Small Grants) Committee. Mick Sharp acknowledges his greatest debt to Jean Williamson, an unpaid but never unappreciated assistant throughout the compilation of this portfolio. We would both thank her for her cartography in the book. We would also both thank Peter Richards at the University Press: he always believed in this book, which was important for us both.